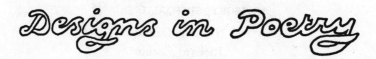

Designs in Poetry

R. STANLEY PETERSON

Formerly, Chairman, English Department
New Trier Township High School
Winnetka, Illinois

MACMILLAN PUBLISHING COMPANY
NEW YORK

COLLIER MACMILLAN PUBLISHERS
LONDON

ACKNOWLEDGMENTS

For permission to use material in this book grateful acknowledgment is made to the following:

George Allen & Unwin, Ltd.: For "The Hammers" from *The Last Blackbird and Other Lines* by Ralph Hodgson.

Chatto & Windus, Ltd.: For "The Groundhog" from *Selected Poems* by Richard Eberhart.

Dodd, Mead & Company: For "The Soldier" from *The Collected Poems of Rupert Brooke*, copyright 1915 by Dodd, Mead & Company, Inc.

Dodd, Mead & Company, The University of New Brunswick, and McClelland and Stewart Ltd.: For "A Vagabond Song" from *Bliss Carman's Poems*, copyright 1929, by Bliss Carman. Reprinted by permission of Dodd, Mead & Company and McClelland and Stewart Ltd., and by special permission of the Bliss Carman Trust, The University of New Brunswick, Canada.

Doubleday & Company, Inc.: For "Waiting" and "Loneliness" by Shiki; "Autumn Nightfall," "Clouds," and "Sent to His Pupil Rensetsu" by Bashō; and "The World Upside Down" by Onitsura from *Introduction to Haiku* by Harold G. Henderson. Copyright © 1958 by Harold G. Henderson. For "fate is unfair" by Don Marquis from *The Lives and Times of Archie and Mehitabel*. Copyright 1918 by Sun Printing & Publishing Association.

E. P. Dutton: For "Indian Sky" from *Selected Poems of Alfred Kreymborg* by Alfred Kreymborg. Copyright © 1945 Alfred Kreymborg. Reprinted by permission of publisher.

Norma Millay Ellis: For "Spring" from *Collected Poems of Edna St. Vincent Millay*, published by Harper & Row. Copyright 1921 and 1948 by Edna St. Vincent Millay. For "Recuerdo" by Edna St. Vincent Millay, from *Collected Poems*, published by Harper & Row. Copyright 1922 and 1950 by Edna St. Vincent Millay.

Faber & Faber Ltd.: For "plato told" and "in Just—" from *Selected Poems* by E. E. Cummings. For "The Express" from *Collected Poems* by Stephen Spender.

Georgia Warm Springs Foundation: For "Rust" by Mary Carolyn Davies, from *Youth Riding*.

Vida L. Guiterman: For "Hills" by Arthur Guiterman, from *The Mirthful Lyre*.

Donald Hall: For "Transcontinent," by Donald Hall, which appeared originally in the *Saturday Review* (April 11, 1959).

Cover design by Jacqui Morgan

Macmillan Publishing Company
866 Third Avenue, New York, New York 10022
Collier Macmillan Canada, Inc.
Printed in the United States of America
ISBN 0-02-194040-1
7 8 9 10 11 12 13   95 94

ACKNOWLEDGMENTS (*continued*)

Harcourt Brace Jovanovich: For "The Beautiful Changes" from *The Beautiful Changes and Other Poems*, copyright, 1947, by Richard Wilbur. Reprinted by permission of Harcourt, Brace & World, Inc. For "plato told" from *Poems 1923–1954* by E. E. Cummings. Copyright, 1944, by E. E. Cummings. For "in Just—" from *Poems 1923–1954* by E. E. Cummings. Copyright, 1923, 1951 by E. E Cummings. For "Caliban in the Coal Mines" from *Challenge* by Louis Untermeyer, copyright, 1914, by Harcourt, Brace & World, Inc.: renewed, 1942, by Louis Untermeyer.

Harper & Row: For "City Evening" from *The Lady is Cold* by E. B. White. Copyright 1929 by Harper & Row. For "Kitchenette Building" from *The World of Gwendolyn Brooks* by Gwendolyn Brooks. Copyright 1945 by Gwendolyn Brooks Blakely. For "That Bright Chimeric Beast" from *On These I Stand* by Countee Cullen. Copyright 1929 by Harper & Brothers; renewed 1957 by Ida M. Cullen.

Holt, Rinehart and Winston, Inc.: For "A Hillside Thaw," "Out, Out—" and "Fire and Ice" by Robert Frost. Copyright 1916, 1921, 1923 by Holt, Rinehart and Winston, Inc. Copyright renewed 1944, 1951 by Robert Frost. For "Prayers of Steel" from *Cornhuskers* by Carl Sandburg. Copyright 1918 by Holt, Rinehart and Winston, Inc. For "Limited" from *Chicago Poems* by Carl Sandburg. Copyright 1916 by Holt, Rinehart and Winston, Inc. Copyright renewed 1944 by Carl Sandburg. For "Loveliest of Trees" and "When I Was One-and-Twenty" from *A Shropshire Lad*—Authorised Edition—from *Complete Poems* by A. E. Housman. Copyright © 1959 by Holt, Rinehart and Winston, Inc.

Edwin Honig and the *Saturday Review*: For "Outer Drive" by Edwin Honig, now appearing in *The Gazabos: Forty-One Poems*, by Edwin Honig, published by Clarke & Way, Inc. First published in the *Saturday Review*, July 7, 1956.

Houghton Mifflin Company: For "The Fish" by Elizabeth Bishop. For "Solitaire" from *The Complete Poetical Works of Amy Lowell*. Reprinted by permission of Houghton Mifflin Company. For "The Ballad of the Oysterman" and "The Chambered Nautilus" by Oliver Wendell Holmes; "The Wreck of the Hesperus" by Henry Wadsworth Longfellow. Reprinted by permission of Houghton Mifflin Company, the original publishers.

Mary Jarrell: For "A Pilot from the Carrier," by Randall Jarrell.

J. B. Lippincott Company: For "When Moonlight Falls" from *Silverhorn* by Hilda Conkling. Copyright 1924, 1952 by Hilda Conkling. Published by J. B. Lippincott Company.

Little, Brown & Company: For "I like to see it lap the miles," and "I never saw a moor" from *The Complete Poems of Emily Dickinson*.

Isabel Garland Lord: For "The Mountains Are a Lonely Folk," by Hamlin Garland.

Macmillan Publishing Co., Inc. For "The Lake Isle of Innisfree" from *Collected Poems* by William Butler Yeats, copyright 1906 by The Macmillan Company, 1934 by William Butler Yeats. For "Abraham Lincoln Walks at Midnight" and "An Indian Summer Day on the Prairie," from *Collected Poems* by Vachel Lindsay, copyright 1914 by The Macmillan Company, 1942 by Elizabeth C. Lindsay.

Edward B. Marks Music: For "The Ballad of Ira Hayes" by Peter LaFarge © copyright Edward B. Marks Music Corporation. Used by permission.

Ellen C. Masters: For "Petit, the Poet" from *Spoon River Anthology* by Edgar Lee Masters. Published by The Macmillan Company.

New Directions: For "A Pact." From Ezra Pound, *Personae*. Copyright 1926, 1954 by Ezra Pound. For "Winter Trees" by William Carlos Williams. Copyright 1938, 1951 by William Carlos Williams. For "Constantly risking absurdity" from Lawrence Ferlinghetti, *A Coney Island of the Mind*. Copyright ©

ACKNOWLEDGMENTS (*continued*)

1958 by Lawrence Ferlinghetti. All reprinted by permission of New Directions Publishing Corporation.

October House, Inc.: For "Frederick Douglass" by Robert Hayden from *Selected Poems*. Copyright © 1966 by Robert Hayden. Reprinted by permission of October House, Inc.

Oxford University Press, Inc.: For "The Groundhog" from *Collected Poems 1930–1960* by Richard Eberhart. Copyright © 1960 by Richard Eberhart.

R. Stanley Peterson: For "Driftwood" by permission of the author.

Laurence Pollinger Limited: For "Fire and Ice," "A Hillside Thaw" and "Out, Out—" from *The Complete Poems of Robert Frost*. Published in the British Commonwealth by Jonathan Cape, Ltd.

Random House, Inc.–Alfred A. Knopf, Inc.: For "To the Stone-Cutters" by Robinson Jeffers, copyright 1924, renewed 1951 by Robinson Jeffers. Reprinted from *The Selected Poetry of Robinson Jeffers* by permission of Random House, Inc. For "Parting Gift" and "Sea Lullaby" from *Collected Poems of Elinor Wylie*, copyright 1932 by Alfred A. Knopf, Inc. Copyright 1920, 1921, 1929, 1932 by Alfred A. Knopf, Inc. For "The Warning" by Adelaide Crapsey from *Verse*, copyright 1915 by Algernon S. Crapsey, renewal copyright 1934 by Adelaide T. Crapsey. For "Yakamochi" and "Akahito," translated by Arthur Waley. For "Fable" and "from The Black Riders" from *Collected Poems* of Stephen Crane, copyright 1930 by Alfred A. Knopf, Inc. For "The Express," copyright 1934 by The Modern Library, Inc. From *Collected Poems 1928–1953* by Stephen Spender, For "Auto Wreck," copyright 1941 by Karl Shapiro, from *Poems 1940–1953* by Karl Shapiro. For Part 3 of "The Interlude," copyright 1944 by Karl Shapiro, from *Poems 1940–1953* by Karl Shapiro. For "On Modern Poetry" by Wallace Stevens. Copyright 1942 by Wallace Stevens. Reprinted from *The Collected Poems of Wallace Stevens*, by permission of Alfred A. Knopf, Inc. For "The Negro Speaks of Rivers" by Langston Hughes. Copyright 1926 by Alfred A. Knopf, Inc. and renewed 1954 by Langston Hughes. Reprinted from *The Weary Blues* by permission of Alfred A. Knopf, Inc. All reprinted by permission of Alfred A. Knopf, Inc. For "An Elementary School Classroom in a Slum," copyright 1942 and renewed 1970 by Stephen Spender. Reprinted from *Selected Poems* by Stephen Spender by permission of Random House, Inc.

Saturday Review: For "Transcontinent," by Donald Hall (April 11, 1959).

Sidgwick & Jackson Ltd.: For "The Soldier" from *The Collected Poems of Rupert Brooke*. Reprinted by permission of the Author's Representatives and of the Publishers, Sidgwick & Jackson Ltd., and McClelland and Stewart Limited.

The Society of Authors: For "Loveliest of Trees" and "When I Was One-and-Twenty" from A. E. Housman's *Collected Poems*. Reprinted by permission of The Society of Authors as the literary representative of the Estate of the late A. E. Housman, and Messrs. Jonathan Cape, Ltd., publishers of A. E. Housman's *Collected Poems*. For "The Listeners" by Walter de la Mare. Reprinted by permission of the Literary Trustees of Walter de la Mare and The Society of Authors as their representative.

The Viking Press: For "Without a Cloak" by Phyllis McGinley from *A Short Walk from the Station*. Copyright 1944 by Phyllis McGinley. For "The Creation" by James Weldon Johnson. From *God's Trombones* by James Weldon Johnson. Copyright 1927 by The Viking Press, Inc., 1955 by Grace Nail Johnson. Reprinted by permission of The Viking Press, Inc.

A. P. Watt & Son, Mrs. Yeats, and Macmillan & Co., Ltd.: For "The Lake Isle of Innisfree" from *Collected Poems of W. B. Yeats*.

Yale University Press: For "Molly Means" from *For My People* by Margaret Walker. Copyright © 1942 by Yale University Press.

Contents

Image, Figure, and Symbol   53

Form and Structure in Poetry   87

CONTENTS

Poems for Study and Enjoyment 145

Reading a Poem

The beauty of a single red rose is often more apparent and vibrant than that of a dozen roses grouped together. The sound of a lone bugle echoing in the stillness of dawn often makes a deeper impression than an entire military band because the listener's senses are totally focused on that solitary instrument. Likewise, the reader who selects a single poem to read frequently has a more meaningful and moving experience than the reader who attempts to read an entire book of poems. In this book, the emphasis is on the study of poems rather than on the study of poetry.

The first group of poems presented in this volume are ballads and narrative forms. These represent the earliest forms of poems, dating back to man's first attempts to communicate through rhythm and sound. Because many of these poems were intended to be sung or chanted, they have a very strong rhythm and definite rhyme pattern. The song-like quality of such poems influenced later poets who tried to incorporate it into their poems. The effects of this influence can be seen in the poems that make up the second section of this book.

According to the nineteenth-century English poet John Keats, lyric poems, which are the kind of poems in the second section of this book, surprise the reader by their "fine excess" of emotion and language. They are expressions of all the excitement, eagerness, sincerity, and feelings that well up within the poet. In addition to appealing to the mind, they are written with a lyrical, or song-like, quality that appeals to the ear. Unless you respond to these qualities, you will not experience these poems as the poets intended.

The poems in the third section of this volume appeal to the imagination. A poet is always seeking a unique way of employing language to create images and convey feelings. In order for you to understand and appreciate these uses of language, you must learn how a poet uses figures of speech and symbols to extend the meaning of a poem.

The fourth section emphasizes the form and structure of poems. Art often consists of taking the ordinary and rearranging it into something that is extraordinary. An artist is someone who has the talent and ability to give shape, form and significance to the commonplace. The poet is an artist who uses the forms of verse to shape his thoughts and express them in an imaginative and striking fashion. The resulting poem is a carefully created unification of feeling and form which evokes a response in the reader.

The creation of a poem begins with an idea in a poet's mind. Sometimes the idea is overtly stated in a poem; sometimes it is so cleverly interwoven within the verse that you must discover it for yourself. The poems in the fifth section challenge you to think in order to find a poet's message. Some of these poems may appear to be deceptively simple at first reading. However, you must remember that some of the most profound ideas can be expressed in the simplest of terms. Frequently a poet finds it more effective to suggest rather than describe the deep emotion he feels. A poem written in this fashion requires a great deal of involvement on your part before you can understand the idea of the poem and respond to its form.

The approximately one hundred fine poems in this book are for the most part supplemented by questions and notes to excite and involve the inquiring mind. These notes and questions help set a purpose and give direction to your study of the poems. However, when you come to the poems in the last section, you will find no questions or notes. You, the reader, are left to examine and enjoy these poems by framing your own questions that will help you experience the poem in its fullest detail.

THE POEM
AS
NARRATIVE

The Poem as Narrative

A good story pleases everyone. Something in the heart of each of us vibrates to the joys and sorrows of others. The excitement of adventure, the ecstasy of suspense—these are some of the pleasures of life, and nowhere are they better described than in the absorbing tales of short story writers and poets.

It is not surprising that the early literature of the world was predominantly narrative. In the days before mass communication, the wandering minstrel and the storyteller were in great demand. They kept alive the glorious deeds of heroes and their warlike bands. The minstrel literally "sang for his supper" as he entertained castle audiences and tavern crowds with his tales of skill and daring, heartsick maidens and fearless lovers.

English folk ballads are a continuation of this early literature. Their themes are the universal themes of popular literature; their subjects are like the dramatic events reported in today's papers: drownings, murders, raids, thefts, hangings, love and marriage. In more recent times, poets have composed new ballads, using the same subjects and much the same form, striving to preserve the naïve but rugged quality of the early folk ballads. Other narrative poets have departed from the ballad form and have written poems that are more personal, more philosophical, and more dramatic, but still strong in their story line.

Read these poems for what they are intended to be: vigorous narratives that give delight because they are warm, personal, and universal.

Barbara Allan

ANONYMOUS

It was in and about the Martinmas ° time,   mid-November
    When the green leaves were a-falling,
That Sir John Graeme in the west country
    Fell in love with Barbara Allan.

He sent his man down through the town,   5
    To the place where she was dwelling,
"O haste and come to my master dear,
    Gin ° ye be Barbara Allan."   if

O hooly,° hooly rose she up   slowly, softly
    To the place where he was lying,   10
And when she drew the curtain by—
    "Young man, I think you're dying."

"O it's I am sick, and very, very sick,
    And 'tis a' for Barbara Allan."
"O the better for me ye's never be,   15
    Tho' your heart's blood were a-spilling.

"O dinna ye mind,° young man," said she,   remember
    "When ye was in the tavern a-drinking,
That ye made the healths gae round and round,
    And slighted Barbara Allan?"   20

He turned his face unto the wall,
    And death was with him dealing:
"Adieu, adieu, my dear friends all,
    And be kind to Barbara Allan."

And slowly, slowly raise she up,   25
    And slowly, slowly left him;
And sighing, said she could not stay,
    Since death of life had reft ° him.   bereft, deprived

She was not gane a mile but two,
    When she heard the dead-bell ringing,   30
And every jow ° that the dead-bell geid,°   stroke; gave
    It cry'd, "Woe to Barbara Allan!"

"O mother, mother, make my bed,
    O make it soft and narrow,
Since my love died for me today,   35
    I'll die for him tomorrow."

1. "Barbara Allan" is a favorite among the old folk ballads. What elements does it contain that almost guarantee its success?
2. Some of the events of the story were omitted, probably because the listeners were so familiar with them. From what you are told, what can you infer? How does the absence of detail affect the pace of the ballad?
3. Roughly half of the lines are made up of dialogue. What is the effect of this use of dialogue?
4. Is Barbara Allan's statement at the end of this poem consistent with the impression given of her in the rest of the ballad? Discuss. Was her treatment of Sir John justified? Explain. Does the poet make any moral judgment of her actions?

The Wife of Usher's Well

ANONYMOUS

There lived a wife at Usher's Well,
    And a wealthy wife was she;
She had three stout and stalwart sons,
    And she sent them o'er the sea.

They hadna been a week from her,   **5**
    A week but barely ane,°   one
Whan word came to the carline wife °   old woman or witch
    That her three sons were gane.°   gone

They hadna been a week from her,
    A week but barely three,   **10**
Whan word came to the carline wife
    That her sons she'd never see.

"I wish the wind may never cease,
    Nor fashes ° in the flood,   troubles, storms
Till my three sons come hame ° to me,   home **15**
    In earthly flesh and blood."

It fell about the Martinmas,
    When nights are lang and mirk,°   dark
The carline wife's three sons came hame,
    And their hats were o' the birk.°   made of birch (a protection **20**
                                       against the living)

It neither grew in syke ° nor ditch,   rivulet
    Nor yet in ony sheugh; °   (pronounced "shuck"), trench
But at the gates o' Paradise,
    That birk grew fair eneugh.°   (rhymes with "shuck")

"Blow up the fire, my maidens!   **25**
    Bring water from the well!
For a' my house shall feast this night,
    Since my three sons are well."

And she had made to them a bed,
    She's made it large and wide;   **30**
And she's ta'en her mantle her about,
    Sat down at the bedside.

Up then crew the red, red cock,
    And up and crew the gray;
The eldest to the youngest said,   **35**
    " 'Tis time we were away."

The cock he hadna craw'd but once,
    And clapp'd his wings at a',°   **all**
When the youngest to the eldest said,
    "Brother, we must awa." °   **away 40**

"The cock doth craw, the day doth daw,°   **dawn**
    The channerin'° worm doth chide;   **fretting, gnawing**
Gin ° we be missed out o' our place,   **if**
    A sair pain we maun bide.°   **we must suffer**

"Fare ye well, my mother dear!   **45**
    Fareweel to barn and byre! °   **cowhouse**
And fare ye weel, the bonny lass
    That kindles my mother's fire."

1. Describe the various scenes of the ballad. How does the poet make you share in the tragedy and grief of the mother and her sons? Is the tone of the ballad hysterical or subdued? How does the tone affect your feeling for the characters?
2. Why do the details of the home, fire, and "bonny lass" make the fate of the boys seem especially sad?

Edward, Edward

ANONYMOUS

"Why dois your brand ° sae drap wi' bluid,°   sword; blood
     Edward, Edward?
Why dois your brand sae drap wi' bluid,
    And why sae sad gang ° yee, O?"   go
"O, I hae killed my hauke sae guid,   5
     Mither, mither,
O, I hae killed my hauke sae guid,
    And I had nae mair ° bot hee, O."   more

"Your haukis ° bluid was nevir sae reid,°   hawk's; red
     Edward, Edward,   10
Your haukis bluid was nevir sae reid,
    My deir son, I tell thee, O."
"O, I hae killed my reid-roan steid,
     Mither, mither,
O, I hae killed my reid-roan steid,   15
    That erst ° was sae fair and frie, O."   once

"Your steid was auld, and ye hae gat mair,
     Edward, Edward,
Your steid was auld, and ye hae gat mair,
    Sum other dule ° ye drie,° O."   sorrow; endure 20
"O, I hae killed my fadir ° deir,   father
     Mither, mither,
O, I hae killed my fadir deir,
    Alas, and wae is mee, O!"

"And whatten penance wul ye drie for that,   25
        Edward, Edward?
And whatten penance wul ye drie for that?
        My deir son, now tell me, O."
"Ile set my feit in yonder boat,
        Mither, mither,   30
Ile set my feit in yonder boat,
        And Ile fare ovir the sea, O."

"And what wul ye doe wi' your towirs and your ha',°   hall
        Edward, Edward?
And what wul ye doe wi' your towirs and your ha',   35
        That were sae fair to see, O?"
"Ile let thame stand tul they doun fa',°   fall
        Mither, mither,
Ile let thame stand tul they doun fa',
        For here nevir mair maun ° I bee, O."   must 40

"And what wul ye leive to your bairns ° and your wife,   children
        Edward, Edward?
And what wul ye leive to your bairns and your wife,
        When ye gang ovir the sea, O?"
"The warldis ° room, late them beg thrae ° life,   world's; through 45
        Mither, mither,
The warldis room, late them beg thrae life,
        For thame nevir mair wul I see, O."

"And what wul ye leive to your ain mither deir,
        Edward, Edward?   50
And what wul ye leive to your ain mither deir?
        My deir son, now tell me, O."
"The curse of hell frae me sall ° ye beir,   shall
        Mither, mither,
The curse of hell frae me sall ye beir,   55
        Sic ° counseils ye gave to me, O."   such

1. What two shocking revelations are made in the ballad?
2. How much of the story is told? What has been left unsaid? One of the concerns of this ballad is to bring you into a sudden and intense encounter with the situation and characters. How does the telling of the story accomplish this?
3. What can be learned about Edward? Is he rich or poor, high born or low? How strong, would you say, has been his mother's influence on him? What is his ultimate response to her? Did you anticipate his reaction toward his wife and children? What might have been the poet's reason for giving this information so suddenly?
4. Describe Edward's mother. What does her questioning reveal about her? What is her attitude toward Edward? How does she respond to his admission of his crime? Does she show surprise? Does she indicate sorrow or remorse? Who, in her opinion, should do penance? What do you learn about her from her question: "And what wul ye leive to your ain mither deir"? From her tone, what does she seem to expect?
5. Suspense is a key element in this ballad. How is it maintained? Try rearranging the stanzas. Does the build-up of suspense suffer? Why is it more appropriate to go from a "hauke" to a "reid-roan steid" than from the "steid" to the "hauke"?
6. Note the repetition in the ballad. What purpose does it serve? Explain, for example, how it acts as a restraint for the wild story told in the ballad. What would be lost if the third and seventh line in each stanza were omitted?
7. Is there in the ballad any condemnation made of Edward or his mother? Review "Barbara Allan." Is there any judgment made of Barbara Allan's treatment of Sir John? On the basis of these two ballads, describe the attitude of the composers of folk ballads (see Glossary, page 174) toward the stories they told.
8. From your reading of these three representative folk ballads, describe the way the story of each is told. What general characteristics of the storytelling technique of ballads can you now give?

Proud Maisie

SIR WALTER SCOTT

Proud Maisie is in the wood,
    Walking so early;
Sweet Robin sits on the bush,
    Singing so rarely.

"Tell me, thou bonny bird,   5
    When shall I marry me?"
"When six braw° gentlemen,   brave
    Kirkward ° shall carry ye."   to church

"Who makes the bridal bed,
    Birdie, say truly?"—   10
"The gray-headed sexton
    That delves the grave duly.

"The glow-worm o'er grave and stone
    Shall light thee steady;
The owl from the steeple sing,   15
    'Welcome, proud lady.' "

1. What answer does the robin give to proud Maisie's question? Does she understand what he is really saying? What is he describing? Show how the details he gives could be related to a marriage ceremony. Who, for example, would the "six braw" men be in the wedding? Look up the archaic meaning for "carry." How could this help to mislead Maisie?
2. How important is the adjective "proud" in this ballad? What is the robin's attitude toward Maisie?

The Wreck of the Hesperus

HENRY WADSWORTH LONGFELLOW

It was the schooner Hesperus,
    That sailed the wintry sea;
And the skipper had taken his little daughtèr,
    To bear him company,

Blue were her eyes as the fairy-flax,   5
    Her cheeks like the dawn of day,
And her bosom white as the hawthorn buds
    That ope in the month of May.

The skipper he stood beside the helm,
    His pipe was in his mouth,   10
And he watched how the veering flaw ° did blow   shifting wind
    The smoke now West, now South.

Then up and spake an old sailòr,
    Had sailed to the Spanish Main,
"I pray thee, put into yonder port,   15
    For I fear a hurricane.

"Last night, the moon had a golden ring,
    And tonight no moon we see!"
The skipper, he blew a whiff from his pipe,
    And a scornful laugh laughed he.   20

Colder and louder blew the wind,
    A gale from the Northeast,

The snow fell hissing in the brine,
    And the billows frothed like yeast.

Down came the storm, and smote amain   25
    The vessel in its strength;
She shuddered and paused, like a frighted steed,
    Then leaped her cable's length.

"Come hither; come hither! my little daughter,
    And do not tremble so;   30
For I can weather the roughest gale
    That ever wind did blow."

He wrapped her warm in his seaman's coat
    Against the stinging blast;
He cut a rope from a broken spar,   35
    And bound her to the mast.

"O father! I hear the church-bells ring,
    Oh say, what may it be?"
" 'Tis a fog-bell on a rock-bound coast!"—
    And he steered for the open sea.   40

"O father! I hear the sound of guns,
    Oh say, what may it be?"
"Some ship in distress, that cannot live
    In such an angry sea!"

"O father! I see a gleaming light,   45
    Oh say, what may it be?"
But the father answered never a word,
    A frozen corpse was he.

Lashed to the helm, all stiff and stark,
    With his face turned to the skies,   50

The lantern gleamed through the gleaming snow
　　On his fixed and glassy eyes.

Then the maiden clasped her hands and prayed
　　That savèd she might be;
And she thought of Christ, who stilled the wave,   55
　　On the Lake of Galilee.

And fast through the midnight dark and drear,
　　Through the whistling sleet and snow,
Like a sheeted ghost, the vessel swept
　　Towards the reef of Norman's Woe.   60

And ever the fitful gusts between
　　A sound came from the land;
It was the sound of the trampling surf,
　　On the rocks and the hard sea-sand.

The breakers were right beneath her bows,   65
　　She drifted a dreary wreck,
And a whooping billow swept the crew
　　Like icicles from her deck.

She struck where the white and fleecy waves
　　Looked soft as carded ° wool,   **combed** 70
But the cruel rocks, they gored her side
　　Like the horns of an angry bull.

Her rattling shrouds, all sheathed in ice,
　　With the masts went by the board; °   **split; went
                                                   over the side**
Like a vessel of glass, she stove and sank,   75
　　Ho! ho! the breakers roared!

At daybreak, on the bleak sea-beach,
　　A fisherman stood aghast,

To see the form of a maiden fair,
　　Lashed close to a drifting mast.　　　　　　　　　80

The salt sea was frozen on her breast,
　　The salt tears in her eyes;
And he saw her hair, like the brown seaweed,
　　On the billows fall and rise.

Such was the wreck of the Hesperus,　　　　　　　85
　　In the midnight and the snow!
Christ save us all from death like this,
　　On the reef of Norman's Woe!

1. The events described in this ballad are tragic. What were the natural causes for the tragedy? Was there anything that might have been done to prevent the wreck of the *Hesperus?* What quality of the skipper was largely responsible for the disaster?
2. How would you describe the daughter? Why do you suppose the poet chose to emphasize her physical characteristics? What response in the reader was the poet attempting to evoke by his description?
3. What was the function of the "old sailor" in the ballad? Is the story of this ballad just the story of a shipwreck or is there a deeper meaning implied? Discuss.
4. Describe the predominant mood of this ballad. What words help to create that mood? What words are particularly effective in helping you to picture the storm and the wreck?
5. The folk ballad "Edward, Edward," like this literary ballad, tells of tragedy. How does the method of storytelling differ in each? Which, for example, makes greater use of dialogue? Which gives a fuller explanation of what has occurred and why it has occurred?

The Glove and the Lions

LEIGH HUNT

King Francis was a hearty king, and loved a royal sport,
And one day, as his lions fought, sat looking on the court.
The nobles fill'd the benches, with the ladies in their pride,
And 'mongst them sat the Count de Lorge, with one for whom
    he sigh'd:
And truly 'twas a gallant thing to see that crowning show,   5
Valor and love, and a king above, and the royal beasts below.

Ramp'd and roar'd the lions, with horrid laughing jaws;
They bit, they glared, gave blows like beams, a wind went with
    their paws;
With wallowing might and stifled roar they roll'd on one another,
Till all the pit with sand and mane was in a thunderous
    smother;   10
The bloody foam above the bars came whisking through the air;
Said Francis then, "Faith, gentlemen, we're better here than
    there."

De Lorge's love o'erheard the King, a beauteous, lively dame,
With smiling lips and sharp bright eyes, which always seem'd the
    same;
She thought, "The Count, my lover, is brave as brave can be;   15
He surely would do wondrous things to show his love of me;
King, ladies, lovers, all look on; the occasion is divine;
I'll drop my glove, to prove ° his love; great glory will   test
    be mine."

She dropp'd her glove, to prove his love, then look'd at him and
    smiled;
He bow'd, and in a moment leap'd among the lions wild;   20
The leap was quick, return was quick, he has regain'd his place,
Then threw the glove, but not with love, right in the lady's face.
"By heaven," said Francis, "rightly done!" and he rose from
    where he sat;
"No love," quoth he, "but vanity, sets love a task like that."

1. Was the outcome of this literary ballad what you expected it to
   be? Why is it a plausible one? Do you agree or disagree with King
   Francis' concluding statement? Why?
2. Which of the characters stands out most clearly in your mind?
   The poet said that the lady had "sharp bright eyes, which always
   seem'd the same." What does this suggest about her character?
3. Typical of the organization of ballads is the breaking down of the
   action into small scenes, concretely described. Show how this is
   done in "The Glove and the Lions." How is the "crowning show"
   described?
4 How does the method of storytelling in this ballad differ from the
   folk ballads you have read? What characteristics does this literary
   ballad share with those folk ballads?

The Ballad of the Oysterman

OLIVER WENDELL HOLMES

It was a tall young oysterman lived by the river-side,
His shop was just upon the bank, his boat was on the tide;
The daughter of a fisherman, that was so straight and slim,
Lived over on the other bank, right opposite to him.

It was the pensive oysterman that saw a lovely maid,   5
Upon a moonlight evening, a-sitting in the shade;
He saw her wave her handkerchief, as much as if to say,
"I'm wide awake, young oysterman, and all the folks away."

Then up arose the oysterman, and to himself said he,
"I guess I'll leave the skiff at home, for fear that folks should
    see;   10
I read it in the story-book, that, for to kiss his dear,
Leander swam the Hellespont,—and I will swim this here."

And he has leaped into the waves, and crossed the shining stream,
And he has clambered up the bank, all in the moonlight gleam;
Oh there were kisses sweet as dew, and words as soft as rain,—   15
But they have heard her father's step, and in he leaps again!

Out spoke the ancient fisherman,—"Oh, what was that, my
    daughter?"
" 'Twas nothing but a pebble, sir, I threw into the water."
"And what is that, pray tell me, love, that paddles off so fast?"
"It's nothing but a porpoise, sir, that's been a-swimming past." 20

Out spoke the ancient fisherman,—"Now bring me my harpoon!
I'll get into my fishing-boat, and fix the fellow soon."
Down fell that pretty innocent, as falls a snow-white lamb,
Her hair drooped round her pallid cheeks, like seaweed on a clam.

Alas for those two loving ones! she waked not from her swound, 25
And he was taken with the cramp, and in the waves was drowned;
But Fate has metamorphosed ° them, in pity of their woe,

           changed
And now they keep an oyster-shop for mermaids down below.

1. How soon in the reading of the poem do you realize that this is
   not a serious poem? Point out the details that give it a humorous
   tone.
2. What would lead you to think that the father knew all the time
   that the porpoise was a young man courting his daughter? In what
   way was the father responsible for what happened?
3. Is suffering a cramp and drowning an appropriate end for a hero?
   Explain.
4. Read in a book of mythology the story of Hero and Leander.
   Knowing their story will help you to understand the humor of this
   poem.

Molly Means

MARGARET WALKER

Old Molly Means was a hag and a witch;
Chile of the devil, the dark, and sitch.
Her heavy hair hung thick in ropes
And her blazing eyes was black as pitch.
Imp at three and wench at 'leben   5
She counted her husbands to the number seben.
    O Molly, Molly, Molly Means
    There goes the ghost of Molly Means.

Some say she was born with a veil on her face
So she could look through unnatchal space   10
Through the future and through the past
And charm a body or an evil place
And every man could well despise
The evil look in her coal black eyes.
    Old Molly, Molly, Molly Means   15
    Dark is the ghost of Molly Means.

And when the tale begun to spread
Of evil and of holy dread:
Her black-hand arts and her evil powers
How she cast her spells and called the dead,　　　　　　20
The younguns was afraid at night
And the farmers feared their crops would blight.
　Old Molly, Molly, Molly Means
　Cold is the ghost of Molly Means.

Then one dark day she put a spell　　　　　　　　　　　25
On a young gal-bride just come to dwell
In the lane just down from Molly's shack
And when her husband come riding back
His wife was barking like a dog
And on all fours like a common hog.　　　　　　　　　30
　O Molly, Molly, Molly Means
　Where is the ghost of Molly Means?

The neighbors come and they went away
And said she'd die before break of day
But her husband held her in his arms　　　　　　　　35
And swore he'd break the wicked charms;
He'd search all up and down the land
And turn the spell on Molly's hand.
　O Molly, Molly, Molly Means
　Sharp is the ghost of Molly Means.　　　　　　　　40

So he rode all day and he rode all night
And at the dawn he come in sight
Of a man who said he could move the spell
And cause the awful thing to dwell
On Molly Means, to bark and bleed   45
Till she died at the hands of her evil deed.
   Old Molly, Molly, Molly Means
   This is the ghost of Molly Means.

Sometimes at night through the shadowy trees
She rides along on a winter breeze.   50
You can hear her holler and whine and cry.
Her voice is thin and her moan is high,
And her cackling laugh or her barking cold
Bring terror to the young and old.
   O Molly, Molly, Molly Means   55
   Lean is the ghost of Molly Means.

1. What similarities do you find between this ballad and the earlier
   folk ballads you have read?
2. This poem was written by an accomplished poet; it is not truly a
   folk ballad. What evidence of professional artistry do you find in
   the language of the poem?
3. The author, Margaret Walker, is one of our more noted black
   poets. How can you tell from the language of the poem that it is
   intended to be a ballad centering around the lives of black people?
4. In which parts of the poem do you find the feelings of horror and
   terror are most effectively evoked? Cite the lines that do so.

The Ballad of Ira Hayes

PETER LA FARGE

This ballad is based on the true story of Ira Hayes, who fought in one of the bloodiest battles in World War II—the battle for the small island of Iwo Jima. The picture of the band of marines raising the American flag on top of Iwo Jima hill was widely published in American newspapers at the time. The ballad accurately describes Ira's subsequent life.

Gather around me people, there's a story I will tell
About a brave young Indian—you should remember well,
From the tribe of the Pima Indians, a proud and noble band,
Who farmed the Phoenix valley in Arizona land.

Chorus:·
Call him drunken Ira Hayes, he won't answer any more   5
Not the whisky drinkin' Indian, nor the marine who went to war.

Down their ditches a thousand years the sparkling water rushed,
Till the white man stole their water rights and the running
    water hushed.
Now Ira's folks were hungry and their land grew crops of weeds,
When war came Ira volunteered, and forgot the white man's
    greed.   10
            [*Chorus*]

There they battled up Iwo Jima hill, two hundred and fifty men,
But only twenty-seven lived to walk back down again;
And when the fight was over and Old Glory raised,
Among the men who held it high was the Indian—Ira Hayes.
            [*Chorus*]

Ira Hayes returned a hero, celebrated through the land,   15
He was wined and speeched and honored, everybody shook his
     hand.
But he was just a Pima Indian—no water, no home, no chance;
At home nobody cared what Ira'd done, and when did Indians
     dance?
                              [Chorus]

Then Ira started drinkin' hard, jail often was his home,
They let him raise the flag and lower it like you'd throw a dog
     a bone.   20
He died drunk early one morning, alone in the land he'd fought
     to save,
Two inches of water in a lonely ditch was the grave for Ira Hayes.
                              [Chorus]

Yeah, call him drunken Ira Hayes
But his land is just as dry,
And his ghost is lyin' thirsty   25
In the ditch where Ira died.

1. This ballad, written within recent years, has been set to music
   and sung by popular singers, most notably by Johnny Cash. How
   can you tell that it was specifically written to be sung?
2. Unlike the older folk ballads, "The Ballad of Ira Hayes" has as its
   purpose more than the telling of a story. It is written to influence
   the thinking of those who read or hear it. What contemporary
   social problem does it deal with? How, through the story it tells
   and through the way it is written, does it seek to influence the
   attitude of readers and listeners with regard to that problem? Cite
   specific parts of the poem that are particularly effective in achiev-
   ing this purpose.

THE POEM
AS
LYRIC

The Poem as Lyric

A lyric poem is the most direct statement of a poet's deepest feeling; it grows out of his conviction that an experience, whether beautiful or painful, is worth expressing, worth communicating. The lyric was originally written to be sung and one of its prevailing characteristics is its melody, its singing quality. What was once achieved by the accompaniment of a musical instrument is now accomplished by a poet's skillful use of the sounds and rhythms of language.

A poet feels experience sharply. He is acutely aware of the world he lives in: the beauty of a summer day, the horrors of war, the love of one person for another, the angers, sorrows, pleasures of everyday living. His art lies in his ability to translate these experiences into words, to experiment with the sounds and rhythms of language until he has his poem.

As you read the poems that follow, you will learn how a poet uses a particular sound to achieve a particular effect; you will see how he uses rhythm to support the sound and meaning of his poem. Read each poem with an open mind. Try to discover what experience brought the poem into being, what the poet is saying, and how he says it.

You will need to recognize some of the technical devices a poet uses in a poem and much of your understanding of these devices will come through the questions after the poem. To help you further is the following brief note on rhythm, which will acquaint you with some of the technical terms you might need to use as you examine the poems in this book.

Remember that much of British and American poetry is strongly rhythmical, with the rhythm most often based on a pattern of stressed and unstressed syllables. This rhythm is measured by working out the repeated units of stressed and unstressed syllables in a given line of poetry. Read the following line and note the way it is marked for stresses.

The Child is fa ther of the Man

The rhythmic pattern of this line is one of four units (called feet), each of which is made up of an unaccented syllable followed by an accented syllable. Further, the rhythm is a duple rhythm, running like a repeated 12121212. Other lines of poetry will show a triple rhythm that runs like a repeated 123123123123; for example:

The Assyr ian came down like the wolf on the fold

The following terms are used to identify the feet most commonly found in poetry. You may need to refer to them as you chart and identify the predominant rhythm patterns of the poems in this book.

iambic . /   as in *above, permit*

trochaic / .   as in *yonder, promise*

dactylic / . .   as in *different, evident*

anapestic . . /   as in *interfere, interrupt*

spondaic / /   as in *daybreak*

pyrrhic . .   as in *on the* (commonly used with the

                        spondee as in *on the dark sea*)

A line of poetry is named by the type of feet and the number of feet it contains. Thus, the line—"The Child is father of the Man"—is called an iambic tetrameter line, a line containing four iambic feet.

The following terms are used to identify the number of feet in a line of poetry:

monometer	one foot	pentameter	five feet
dimeter	two feet	hexameter	six feet
trimeter	three feet	heptameter	seven feet
tetrameter	four feet	octameter	eight feet

Often a poet will use a combination of feet in a poem. As you read more poems, you will become increasingly aware of the wide varieties of rhythm patterns used.

A Vagabond Song

BLISS CARMAN

There is something in the autumn that is native to my blood—
Touch of manner, hint of mood;
And my heart is like a rhyme,
With the yellow and the purple and the crimson keeping time.

The scarlet of the maple can shake me like a cry   5
Of bugles going by.
And my lonely spirit thrills
To see the frosty asters like a smoke upon the hills.

There is something in October sets the gypsy blood astir;
We must rise and follow her,   10
When from every hill of flame
She calls and calls each vagabond by name.

1. What does the word *vagabond* connote to you? How would you
   describe a vagabond? What details in the poem suggest the vitality
   of such a person? What is the "something in the autumn" that
   makes the speaker want to "follow her"?
2. Try to experience the surging movement of this poem. Look at the
   pattern of the lines. How is the free-roaming spirit of the vagabond
   suggested by the lines of the poem? What is the effect of positioning the long first and last lines of each stanza against the shorter
   middle lines? What emotion does this poem convey?

Song

ROBERT BROWNING

The year's at the spring
The day's at the morn;
Morning's at seven;
The hillside's dew-pearled;
The lark's on the wing;   5
The snail's on the thorn:
God's in his heaven—
All's right with the world!
      —from *Pippa Passes*

1. What is the emotion expressed in this poem? The speaker in this poem is a little girl, Pippa. Of what is she singing? Consider the three images used to convey the beauty of the morning. What is the effect of the third image on the poem?
2. The poem concludes with a general comment describing Pippa's attitude toward the world. Is this comment in keeping with the rest of the poem? Explain.
3. Scan this poem. Notice the numerous triple rhythms. What effect do they have on the pace of the poem?

My Heart Leaps Up

WILLIAM WORDSWORTH

My heart leaps up when I behold
   a rainbow in the sky:
So was it when my life began;
So is it now I am a man;
So be it when I shall grow old,   5
   Or let me die!
The Child is father of the Man;
And I could wish my days to be
Bound each to each by natural piety.

1. What is the speaker's response to nature—as expressed in line 1?
   Is it an intellectual response? A spontaneous response? Explain.
   What is the relation between this response and the wish the speaker
   expresses in the last two lines? What does Wordsworth mean by
   "natural piety"? ·
2. Line 7 expresses a paradox—an apparent contradiction. How could
   a child be father of the man? In the light of lines 3-6, try to explain
   the paradox. What continuing process, what continuity is the
   speaker describing?
3. The basic foot in this poem is iambic, the basic meter is tetrameter.
   What variations of this pattern does the poet use? Why is line 6
   so short? What is the effect of this line on the rhythm and meaning of the poem?

The Creation

JAMES WELDON JOHNSON

And God stepped out on space,
And He looked around and said:
I'm lonely—
I'll make me a world.

And far as the eye of God could see   5
Darkness covered everything,
Blacker than a hundred midnights
Down in a cypress swamp.

Then God smiled,
And the light broke,   10
And the darkness rolled up on one side,
And the light stood shining on the other,
And God said: That's good!

Then God reached out and took the light in His hands,
And God rolled the light around in His hands   15
Until He made the sun;

And He set that sun a-blazing in the heavens.
And the light that was left from making the sun
God gathered it up in a shining ball
And flung it against the darkness,   20
Spangling the night with the moon and stars.
Then down between

The darkness and the light
He hurled the world;
And God said: That's good!   25

Then God himself stepped down—
And the sun was on His right hand,
And the moon was on His left;
The stars were clustered about His head,
And the earth was under His feet.   30
And God walked, and where He trod
His footsteps hollowed the valleys out
And bulged the mountains up.

Then He stopped and looked and saw
That the earth was hot and barren.   35
So God stepped over to the edge of the world
And He spat out the seven seas—
He batted His eyes, and the lightnings flashed—
He clapped His hands, and the thunders rolled—
And the waters above the earth came down,   40
The cooling waters came down.

Then the green grass sprouted,
And the little red flowers blossomed,
The pine tree pointed his finger to the sky,
And the oak spread out his arms,   45
The lakes cuddled down in the hollows of the ground,
And the rivers ran down to the sea;
And God smiled again,
And the rainbow appeared,
And curled itself around His shoulder.   50

Then God raised His arm and He waved His hand
Over the sea and over the land,
And He said: Bring forth! Bring forth!

And quicker than God could drop His hand,
Fishes and fowls 55
And beasts and birds
Swam the rivers and the seas,
Roamed the forests and the woods,
And split the air with their wings.
And God said: That's good! 60

Then God walked around,
And God looked around
On all that He had made.
He looked at His sun,
And He looked at His moon, 65
And He looked at His little stars;
He looked on His world
With all its living things,
And God said: I'm lonely still.

Then God sat down— 70
On the side of a hill where He could think;
By a deep, wide river He sat down;
With His head on His hands,
God thought and thought,
Till He thought: I'll make me a man! 75

Up from the bed of the river
God scooped the clay;
And by the bank of the river
He kneeled Him down;
And there the great God Almighty 80
Who lit the sun and fixed it in the sky,
Who flung the stars to the most far corner of the night,
Who rounded the earth in the middle of His hand;
This Great God,
Like a mammy bending over her baby, 85

Kneeled down in the dust
Toiling over a lump of clay
Till He shaped it in His own image;

Then into it He blew the breath of life,
And man became a living soul.   90
Amen. Amen.

1. There is excitement in this poem and a sense of the dramatic. What causes this effect? Show, for example, how the poem rises to great climaxes and then diminishes to passages that are soft and gentle.
2. Notice that no rhyme has been used. How is a melodious effect achieved without the aid of rhyme? What use is made of repetition? What is the effect of the repetition?
3. This poem imitates the spirit and fervor of the old-time evangelical preachers. What qualities does it share with their sermons?
4. If you have a King James Bible available, read a portion of Genesis. What similarities can you find with Johnson's poem?

Meeting at Night

ROBERT BROWNING

The gray sea and the long black land;
And the yellow half-moon large and low;
And the startled little waves that leap
In fiery ringlets from their sleep,
As I gain the cove with pushing prow,   5
And quench its speed i' the slushy sand.

Then a mile of warm sea-scented beach;
Three fields to cross till a farm appears;
A tap at the pane, the quick sharp scratch
And blue spurt of a lighted match,   10
And a voice less loud, through its joys and fears,
Than the two hearts beating each to each!

1. Describe what took place before the meeting. When were you able
   to tell that this was a love poem?
2. What is the mood or atmosphere of the poem? What helps to
   create it?
3. Read the poem aloud, noting the stressed words. Although the
   rhythm is quite irregular, many of the lines contain four accents.
   What is the effect of this rhythm? What feeling do you get as you
   read the poem?
4. One of the great values of poetry is that it implies more than it
   states. Point out examples in this poem.

Hills

ARTHUR GUITERMAN

I never loved your plains;—
    Your gentle valleys,
Your drowsy country lanes
    And pleached ° alleys.   interwoven, twisted, winding

I want my hills!—the trail   5
    That scorns the hollow.
Up, up the ragged shale
    Where few will follow.

Up, over wooded crest
    And mossy boulder   10
With strong thigh, heaving chest,
    And swinging shoulder.

So let me hold my way,
    By nothing halted,
Until at close of day   15
    I stand, exalted.

High on my hills of dream—
    Dear hills that know me!
And then, how fair will seem
    The lands below me.   20

How pure, at vesper-time,
    The far bells ringing!
God, give me hills to climb,
    And strength for climbing!

1. Sometimes the rhymed syllables are the last syllables; for example, *plains* and *lanes* in lines 1 and 3. Such a rhyme is said to be masculine. Sometimes the rhymed syllables are followed by one or more unaccented syllables which are identical in sound; for example, *valleys* and *alleys* in lines 2 and 4. Such a rhyme is said to be feminine. Find other examples of both rhymes in this poem.
2. Pick out and identify the predominant rhythm of the poem. Study exceptions in lines 7, 9, 11, 17, 22, 23. Try to account for the shift of rhythm in each of these lines.
3. Discuss how much the singing quality of this poem is due to the idea of the poem, and how much it is due to the rhythm, the rhyme, and the sound of the individual words.
4. Compare this poet's attitude toward hills with the following poet's attitude toward mountains.

The Mountains Are a Lonely Folk

HAMLIN GARLAND

The mountains they are silent folk,
    They stand afar—alone;
And the clouds that kiss their brows at night
    Hear neither sigh nor groan.
Each bears him in his ordered place   5
    As soldiers do, and bold and high
They fold their forests round their feet
    And bolster up the sky.

from *Song of the Open Road*

WALT WHITMAN

Afoot and light-hearted I take to the open road,
Healthy, free, the world before me,
The long brown path before me leading wherever I choose.

Henceforth I ask not good-fortune, I myself am good-fortune,
Henceforth I whimper no more, postpone no more, need
    nothing,   5
Done with indoor complaints, libraries, querulous °   whining
    criticisms,
Strong and content I travel the open road

1. These lines reveal the poet's desire for a certain way of life. Does he
   mean only that he wishes to travel from place to place, or is he
   expressing a particular attitude toward life? Explain. What is he
   most anxious to leave behind?
2. Characterize the speaker of this poem. What words especially reveal him? Is he hesitant about the way he makes his statement to
   the world? How would you describe the tone of this poem—that is,
   the speaker's attitude toward what he is saying?
3. Whitman made no use here of rhyme or regular rhythm. He has
   written this poem in *free verse*. Why is this form particularly
   appropriate for his poem?

The Lake Isle of Innisfree

WILLIAM BUTLER YEATS

I will arise and go now, and go to Innisfree,
And a small cabin build there, of clay and wattles made;
Nine bean rows will I have there, a hive for the honey bee,
    And live alone in the bee-loud glade.

And I shall have some peace there, for peace comes dropping
    slow,   5
Dropping from the veils of the morning to where the cricket
    sings;
There midnight's all a glimmer, and noon a purple glow,
    And evening full of the linnet's wings.

I will arise and go now, for always night and day
I hear lake water lapping with low sounds by the shore;   10
While I stand on the roadway, or on the pavements gray,
    I hear it in the deep heart's core.

Daffodils

WILLIAM WORDSWORTH

I wandered lonely as a cloud
    That floats on high o'er vales and hills,
When all at once I saw a crowd,
    A host, of golden daffodils;

Beside the lake, beneath the trees,   5
Fluttering and dancing in the breeze.

Continuous as the stars that shine
    And twinkle on the Milky Way,
They stretched in never-ending line
    Along the margin of a bay: 10
Ten thousand saw I at a glance,
Tossing their heads in sprightly dance.

The waves beside them danced; but they
    Outdid the sparkling waves in glee:
A poet could not but be gay,   15
    In such a jocund ° company: joyful
I gazed—and gazed—but little thought
What wealth the show to me had brought:

For oft, when on my couch I lie
    In vacant or in pensive mood,   20
They flash upon that inward eye
    Which is the bliss of solitude;
And then my heart with pleasure fills,
And dances with the daffodils.

1. As you read these two lyrics, you will be aware of their melodious-
   ness. Can you suggest what contributes to their music? Consider,
   for example, the repetition of similar vowel sounds (see *assonance*,
   in Glossary, page 174) that occurs within various lines in each
   poem. Read lines 1-2 of "Daffodils" and note how the open "o"
   sound imitates the free movement of a cloud. Find other examples
   of assonance in these poems.
2. How would you describe the mood of each poem? Is the occasion
   of the poem the same in each case? What does the speaker in
   Yeats's poem long for? Does Wordsworth express a similar need in
   his poem or is his experience a different one? Discuss fully.

Home-Thoughts, from Abroad

ROBERT BROWNING

Oh, to be in England
Now that April's there,
And whoever wakes in England
Sees, some morning, unaware,
That the lowest boughs and the brushwood sheaf 5
Round the elm-tree bole ° are in tiny leaf,   trunk
While the chaffinch sings on the orchard bough
In England—now!

And after April, when May follows,
And the whitethroat builds, and all the swallows! 10
Hark, where my blossomed pear-tree in the hedge
Leans to the field and scatters on the clover
Blossoms and dewdrops—at the bent spray's edge—
That's the wise thrush; he sings each song twice over,
Lest you should think he never could recapture 15
The first fine careless rapture!
And though the fields look rough with hoary dew,
All will be gay when noontide wakes anew
The buttercups, the little children's dower
    Far brighter than this gaudy melon-flower! 20

1. What is the occasion for this poem? Look for clues in the title
   and in lines 1, 2, and 20. What country is suggested by "melon-
   flower"?

2. What is the poet's feeling about what he is describing? How do you
   know that what he describes has a special meaning for him?
3. Note that the lines of the poem become longer as the poem pro-
   gresses. How does this change support the meaning of the lines?
4. What poetic foot occurs most frequently in this poem?

How Do I Love Thee?

ELIZABETH BARRETT BROWNING

How do I love thee? Let me count the ways.
I love thee to the depth and breadth and height
My soul can reach, when feeling out of sight
For the ends of Being and ideal Grace.
I love thee to the level of everyday's   5
Most quiet need, by sun and candlelight.
I love thee freely, as men strive for Right;
I love thee purely, as they turn from Praise.
I love thee with the passion put to use
In my old griefs, and with my childhood's faith.   10
I love thee with a love I seemed to lose
With my lost saints—I love thee with the breath,
Smiles, tears, of all my life!—and, if God choose,
I shall but love thee better after death.

1. There are no fewer than seven attempts in this poem to describe
   the quality of a person's love. Try to explain each in your own
   words.
2. What is the effect of the repetition of "I love thee"?
3. Study the rhymes. Which seem to you less than perfect?

A Red, Red Rose

ROBERT BURNS

O, my luve is like a red, red rose,
    That's newly sprung in June.
O, my luve is like the melodie,
    That's sweetly played in tune.

As fair art thou, my bonie lass,   5
    So deep in luve am I,
And I will luve thee still, my dear,
    Till a' the seas gang dry.

Till a' the seas gang dry, my dear,
    And the rocks melt wi' the sun!   10
And I will luve thee still, my dear,
    While the sands o' life shall run.

And fare thee weel, my only luve,
    And fare thee weel a while!
And I will come again, my luve,   15
    Tho' it were ten thousand mile!

1. Robert Burns is famous for the many songs he wrote—songs filled with energy and joy, as is this expression of love. As you read it, consider the effect of the simple diction, the length of the lines, the repetition, the lilting "l" sounds in the poem. How do these elements work to create the melodious quality of the poem?
2. Note the hyperbole (exaggeration) in line 8. Point out other examples of hyperbole. Does such exaggeration make you doubt the sincerity of the singer? Does the music of the lines carry conviction? What can you tell about the singer?

Recuerdo

EDNA ST. VINCENT MILLAY

We were very tired, we were very merry—
We had gone back and forth all night on the ferry.
It was bare and bright, and smelled like a stable—
But we looked into a fire, we leaned across a table,
We lay on a hill-top underneath the moon;   5
And the whistles kept blowing, and the dawn came soon.

We were very tired, we were very merry—
We had gone back and forth all night on the ferry;
And you ate an apple, and I ate a pear,
From a dozen of each we had bought somewhere;   10
And the sky went wan, and the wind came cold,
And the sun rose dripping, a bucketful of gold.

We were very tired, we were very merry,
We had gone back and forth all night on the ferry.
We hailed, "Good-morrow, mother!" to a shawl-covered head, 15
And bought a morning paper, which neither of us read;
And she wept, "God bless you!" for the apples and pears,
And we gave her all our money but our subway fares.

1. *Recuerdo* is a Spanish word meaning "remembrance." Why is
   this an appropriate title for this poem? What do the many things
   remembered tell you about the speaker?

2. What are the two different feelings mentioned in line 1? Consider, too, the terms in which Miss Millay describes the ferry. Why do you think the speaker would be so quick to introduce the pleasant association of line 4 after the not so pleasant association of line 3? Find other examples of contrasting feelings or impressions in the poem. Referring to the poem for your evidence, give your opinion about the speaker's attitude toward the experience she described.

3. Chart the rhyme scheme. You will soon note that the poem is made up of couplets (see Glossary, page 174). Consider the rhymes and note their relative simplicity. Some, like "moon"—"soon," are almost a cliché. Why do you suppose the poet chose such a rhyme scheme for this poem? How is it appropriate to the statement of the poem?

4. Read the poem aloud. The rhythm is irregular but you will be aware of the pattern of strong stresses in each line. How does the somewhat sing-song quality of the rhythm support or contribute to the tone of the poem?

Eldorado

EDGAR ALLAN POE

Gaily bedight,°   decked out
  A gallant knight,
In sunshine and in shadow,
  Had journeyed long,
  Singing a song,   5
In search of Eldorado.

But he grew old,
  This knight so bold,
And o'er his heart a shadow
    Fell as he found   10
  No spot of ground
That looked like Eldorado.

  And, as his strength
  Failed him at length,
He met a pilgrim shadow: 15
    "Shadow," said he,
  "Where can it be,
This land of Eldorado?"

  "Over the Mountains
  Of the Moon,   20
Down the Valley of the Shadow,
    Ride, boldly ride,"
  The shade replied,
"If you seek for Eldorado!"

1. Poets are enthusiastic about ideals, about love, about country, about friendship—about many things. What does "Eldorado" stand for in this poem? Look up the derivation of the name in a good dictionary.
2. What is the meaning of the shadow's advice to the knight, "Ride, boldly ride'?
3. Melody in poetry is a result of rhyme, alliteration, and the repetition of appropriate vowel and consonant sounds. *Alliteration* is the repetition of initial consonant sounds. *Assonance,* as you have read, is the repetition of vowel sounds. Study the pleasing effects produced in "Eldorado" by Poe's use of these devices.

An Elementary School Classroom in a Slum

STEPHEN SPENDER

Far far from gusty waves, these children's faces.
Like rootless weeds the torn hair round their paleness.
The tall girl with her weighed-down head. The paper-seeming
    boy with rat's eyes. The stunted unlucky heir
Of twisted bones, reciting a father's gnarled disease,   5
His lesson from his desk. At back of the dim class,
One unnoted, sweet and young: his eyes live in a dream
Of squirrels' game, in tree room, other than this.

On sour cream walls, donations. Shakespeare's head
Cloudless at dawn, civilized dome riding all cities.   10
Belled, flowery, Tyrolese° valley. Open-handed map
Awarding the world its world. And yet, for these
Children, these windows, not this world, are world,
Where all their future's painted with a fog,
A narrow street sealed in with a lead sky,   15
Far far from rivers, capes, and stars of words.

Surely Shakespeare is wicked, the map a bad example
With ships and sun and love tempting them to steal—
For lives that slyly turn in their cramped holes
From fog to endless night? On their slag heap, these children   20
Wear skins peeped through by bones and spectacles of steel
With mended glass, like bottle bits on stones.
All of their time and space are foggy slum
So blot their maps with slums as big as doom.

                          beautiful region of the Alps

Unless, governor, teacher, inspector, visitor,   25
This map becomes their window and these windows
That open on their lives like crouching tombs
Break, O break open, till they break the town
And show the children to the fields and all their world
Azure on their sands, to let their tongues   30
Run naked into books, the white and green leaves open
The history theirs whose language is the sun.

1. The poem begins with a picture of typical students in a slum
   classroom, the picture being expressed through similes and metaphors. What feeling about the school children do you get from
   the different images in lines 1-8?
2. Stanza 2, describing the classroom and its environment, further
   develops a feeling in the reader about these children and their
   world, this time through a contrast. What is this contrast? What
   feeling does this contrast create in the reader?
3. Why, according to the speaker, may the bust of Shakespeare and
   the map of the world in the room be "a bad example" for these
   children? Which images in the third stanza further intensify our
   impression of the conditions in which these children exist?
4. In the last stanza the speaker seizes his earlier images of the map
   and the classroom windows to create a new feeling about these
   children and their future. Show how this feeling is first expressed,
   and how the poet's language and images in the last part of the
   poem make the emotion stronger and stronger. Discuss specifically
   the implications of the images in the last five lines.
5. This poem was written a number of years ago. To what degree is
   it still appropriate in our society? Illustrate its appropriateness
   either through your personal knowledge or knowledge you may
   have gained from reading or other sources.

IMAGE,
FIGURE,
AND SYMBOL

Image, Figure, and Symbol

Through our senses we take in the world around us and through language we record our impressions. We see, we hear, we feel, we smell, we touch—and who knows how many more senses we use that the psychologists are only beginning to explore! Since one of the most appealing aspects of poetry is its calling upon our imagination to experience these sensations with the poet, we must open our "reading eye" to the poet's images. We must see the flash of color, hear the clash of armor, feel the skin of the toad, smell the ocean, and touch the underbelly of the snake. Otherwise the poet's experiences will not become our experiences.

More difficult is our recognition of the figurative power of language. Everyday speech is filled with this phenomenon; our slang overflows with similes, metaphors, personifications, irony, and all of the many forms of figurative expression. But the poet is more subtle; his comparisons are more perceptive and more daring. His meanings are sometimes difficult to understand because the figure of speech goes beyond the experience of the reader or reduces the thought of the poet into such a compressed package that the reader cannot understand all that the poet means. Through the figure of speech, the poet intends to clarify his meaning. Death, for example, is an abstract idea. So are honor, justice, and beauty. Definitions are not very helpful in explaining what death is like, how honor demonstrates itself, when justice exists, what beauty is. The poet, faced with the problem of making these abstractions concrete, expresses his meaning in figurative language, and thus indirectly shows you his truths.

Robert Louis Stevenson, in his poem "Requiem," tells in the first stanza that he accepts the idea of death:

Under the wide and starry sky,
Dig the grave and let me lie.
Glad did I live and gladly die,
And I laid me down with a will.

The imagery is here, but there is no convincing statement about death until you reach the second stanza. What did he mean by "with a will"? You are not sure until he draws a comparison between himself and the sailor, between himself and the hunter.

This be the verse you grave° for me: engraved
Here he lies where he longed to be,
Home is the sailor, home from the sea,
And the hunter home from the hill.

Since you know pretty well how the hunter and the sailor feel upon their return home from dangerous and tiring journeys, you can transfer that feeling to the poet's feeling about death. Now you know what he means by "with a will." Thus the figurative language enlightens the emotion, makes clear the inexplicable.

In the poems of this section you will be able to recognize uses of language which are different from those encountered in straightforward prose. The names of the figures of speech, the nature of irony and symbol, will become apparent from the reading of the poems and from your study of the notes and questions. Begin your reading with a curiosity about language, and your awakened awareness will bring you more exciting reading than you have known before.

When Moonlight Falls

HILDA CONKLING

When moonlight falls on the water
It is like fingers touching the chords of a harp
On a misty day.
When moonlight strikes the water
I cannot get it into my poem: 5
I only hear the tinkle of ripplings of light.
When I see the water's fingers and the moon's rays
Intertwined,
I think of all the words I love to hear,
And try to find words white enough   10
For such shining. . . .

1. The poet has attempted to capture in words an intense sensory experience; that is, to create an image. What natural phenomenon did she observe? It was primarily a visual experience, but did she appeal only to the sense of sight in her poem? To which other senses did she appeal? She does not describe the experience literally. Did you, however, get a feeling of what she saw?
2. What comparison is made in the first three lines of the poem? Is this simile continued throughout the poem or does it change? What is the dilemma the poet describes in this poem? What does she mean by "words white enough"?

Indian Sky

ALFRED KREYMBORG

The old squaw
is one
with the old stone behind her.
Both have squatted there—
ask mesa   5
or mountain how long?
... the bowl she holds—
clay ritual of her faith—
is one
with the thought of the past;   10
and one with the now;
... the earth holds her
as she holds the bowl—
ask kiva°   underground Pueblo ceremonial room
or shrine how much longer?   15
No titan
or destroyer,
or future thought,
can part
earth and this woman,   20
woman and bowl:
the same shawl
wraps them around.

1. This poem is like a painting; it presents a strong visual image.
   Describe in detail what you might see if this picture were depicted
   on canvas. Include in your description the feelings the painting
   might evoke in the spectator.
2. Where in this poem do you find symbols suggested? What con-
   ception of the American Indian is developed in this poem?

Haiku

Waiting
Night; and once again,
    the while I wait for you, cold wind
        turns into rain.

—Shiki

Autumn Nightfall
On a withered branch
    a crow has settled—
        autumn nightfall.

—Bashō

Loneliness
No sky at all;
    no earth at all—and still
        the snowflakes fall. . . .

—Shiki

Clouds
Clouds·come from time to time—
    and bring to men a chance to rest
        from looking at the moon.

—Bashō

Sent to His Pupil Rensetsu
Won't you come and see
   loneliness? Just one leaf
      from the *kiri* tree.
                                          —Bashō

The World Upside Down
The trout leaps high—
   below him, in the river bottom,
      clouds fly by.
                                          —Onitsura

By way of pretext
I said "I will go
And look at
The condition of the bamboo fence";
But it was really to see you!
                                          —Yakamochi

The men of valor
Have gone to the honorable hunt:
The ladies
Are trailing their red petticoats
Over the clean sea-beach.
                                          —Akahito

1. The haiku are short, simple poems which are rich in suggestion.
   Through imagery and implication they say much in little space.
2. Discuss the appropriateness of the imagery.
3. The last two poems are "tankas," similar to haiku but having five
   lines. Suggest a title for each tanka that you think best expresses
   the idea, mood, or experience of each poem.

An Indian Summer Day
on the Prairie

VACHEL LINDSAY

In the Beginning
The sun is a huntress young,
The sun is red, red joy,
The sun is an Indian girl,
Of the tribe of the Illinois.

Mid-morning
The sun is a smoldering fire,   5
That creeps through the high gray plain,
And leaves not a bush of cloud
To blossom with flowers of rain.

Noon
The sun is a wounded deer,
That treads pale grass in the skies,   10
Shaking his golden horns,
Flashing his baleful eyes.

Sunset
The sun is an eagle old;
There in the windless west,
Atop of the spirit-cliffs   15
He builds him a crimson nest.

1. Through a series of metaphors, the poet describes the many changes in the sun as it moves across the sky in a day. Discuss the effectiveness of the imagery. Is each word used consistent with the basic image of the stanza? Why are the pictures that Lindsay paints of the movement of the sun richer than a prose statement would be?
2. Which metaphor seems to you the most effective? Why?

The Eagle

ALFRED, LORD TENNYSON

He clasps the crag with crooked hands;
Close to the sun in lonely lands,
Ringed with the azure world, he stands.

The wrinkled sea beneath him crawls;
He watches from his mountain walls,   5
And like a thunderbolt he falls.

1. Is there physical movement described in the first three lines? What is the image presented? What is the effect of "hands" in line 1 instead of "claws"? What is the impression of the eagle that you get from this stanza?
2. What comment does the poet make on the world of men in line 4? Consider, for example, the words *wrinkled* and *crawled*. What added impression do you get of the eagle from line 6? How does the placing of "he stands" and "he falls" contribute to the poem?
3. Pick out examples of alliteration, simile, and metaphor.

Fog

LIZETTE WOODWORTH REESE

What grave has cracked and let this frail thing out,
To press its poor face to the window-pane;
Or, head hid in frayed cloak, to drift about
The mallow bush, then out to the wet lane?
Long-closeted scents across the drippings break,   5
Of violet petunias blowing there,
A shred of mint, mixed with whatever ache
Old springs have left behind wedged tight in air.
Small, aged things peer in, ready to slip
Into the chairs, and watch and stare apace;   10
The house has loosened from its grasp of yore
Dark-horded tales. Were I, finger on lip,
To climb the stair, might I not find the place
Turned all to huddled shape, white on the floor?

1. Trace the imagery from "frail thing" to "poor face" to "frayed cloak." What picture and mood are evoked by the series of metaphors? What senses are appealed to?
2. What are the "aged things" that peer in?
3. What do you make of the last three lines?
4. Does the title indicate the subject of the poem or does it symbolize the poet's impressions and recollections? Explain. Why wouldn't "Ghosts" or "A Haunted House" have served as well as a title?
5. Which images convey a sense of the past? Which create the mood of the poem?

Solitaire

AMY LOWELL

When night drifts along the streets of the city,
And sifts down between the uneven roofs,
My mind begins to peek and peer.
It plays at ball in old, blue Chinese gardens,
And shakes wrought dice-cups in Pagan temples,   5
Amid the broken flutings of white pillars.
It dances with purple and yellow crocuses in its hair,
And its feet shine as they flutter over drenched grasses.
How light and laughing my mind is,
When all the good folk have put out their bed-room candles,   10
And the city is still!

1. What is the meaning of line 3? Why is night an especially good
   time for a poet to "peek and peer"? Where does the poet's mind
   take her? Examine the images in lines 4-8. What makes them so
   vivid?
2. Explain the title of the poem. What do you think was the poet's
   mood as she wrote this poem? What words help to convey this
   mood? How would you describe the atmosphere of the city? What
   do words like *drifts* and *sifts* suggest?
3. What is the difference between the poet and "all the good folk"
   who are mentioned in line 10? What might Miss Lowell be im-
   plying about the special faculties of the poet? Do you agree with
   her? Or do you think she makes the poet more special than she
   should?

A Hillside Thaw

ROBERT FROST

To think to know the country and not know
The hillside on the day the sun lets go
Ten million silver lizards out of snow!
As often as I've seen it done before
I can't pretend to tell the way it's done. 5
It looks as if some magic of the sun
Lifted the rug that bred them on the floor
And the light breaking on them made them run.
But if I thought to stop the wet stampede,
And caught one silver lizard by the tail, 10
And put my foot on one without avail,
And threw myself wet-elbowed and wet-kneed
In front of twenty others' wriggling speed,—
In the confusion of them all aglitter,
And birds that joined in the excited fun 15
By doubling and redoubling song and twitter,
I have no doubt I'd end by holding none.

It takes the moon for this. The sun's a wizard
By all I tell; but so's the moon a witch.
From the high west she makes a gentle cast 20
And suddenly, without a jerk or twitch,
She has her spell on every single lizard.
I fancied when I looked at six o'clock
The swarm still ran and scuttled just as fast.
The moon was waiting for her chill effect. 25
I looked at nine; the swarm was turned to rock
In every lifelike posture of the swarm,

Transfixed on mountain slopes almost erect.
Across each other and side by side they lay.
The spell that so could hold them as they were   30
Was wrought through trees without a breath of storm
To make a leaf, if there had been one, stir.
It was the moon's: she held them until day,
One lizard at the end of every ray.
The thought of my attempting such a stay!   35

1. What kind of person was observing the magic of the sun? Why
   were his efforts to stop it "without avail"?
2. What does "this" stand for in line 18? What does "it" represent
   in line 33? What natural explanation could be given of the event
   described in this fanciful way? Which is the more effective? Why?
   Why was the image of the lizards so effective?

The Fish

ELIZABETH BISHOP

I caught a tremendous fish
and held him beside the boat
half out of water, with my hook
fast in a corner of his mouth.
He didn't fight.   5
He hadn't fought at all.
He hung a grunting weight,
battered and venerable
and homely. Here and there
his brown skin hung in strips   10
like ancient wallpaper,

and its pattern of darker brown
was like wallpaper:
shapes like full-blown roses
stained and lost through age. 15
He was speckled with barnacles,
fine rosettes of lime,
and infested
with tiny white sea-lice,
and underneath two or three 20
rags of green weed hung down.
While his gills were breathing in
the terrible oxygen
—the frightening gills
fresh and crisp with blood, 25
that can cut so badly—
I thought of the coarse white flesh
packed in like feathers,
the big bones and the little bones,
the dramatic reds and blacks 30
of his shiny entrails,
and the pink swim-bladder
like a big peony.
I looked into his eyes
which were far larger than mine 35
but shallower, and yellowed,
the irises backed and packed
with tarnished tinfoil
seen through the lenses
of old scratched isinglass. 40
They shifted a little, but not
to return my stare.
—It was more like the tipping
of an object toward the light.
I admired his sullen face, 45
the mechanism of his jaw,
and then I saw
that from his lower lip

—if you could call it a lip—
grim, wet, and weaponlike,   50
hung five old pieces of fish-line,
or four and a wire leader
with the swivel still attached,
and with all their five big hooks
grown firmly in his mouth.   55
A green line, frayed at the end
where he broke it, two heavier lines,
and a fine black thread
still crimped from the strain and snap
when it broke and he got away.   60
Like medals with their ribbons
frayed and wavering,
a five-haired beard of wisdom
trailing from his aching jaw.
I stared and stared   65
and victory filled up
the little rented boat,
from the pool of bilge
where oil had spread a rainbow
around the rusted engine   70
to the bailer rusted orange,
the sun-cracked thwarts,°   seats or braces
the oarlocks on their strings,
the gunnels °—until everything   (gunwales), the inside rim
was rainbow, rainbow, rainbow!   of the small boat   75
And I let the fish go.

1. Select what you consider the most striking images and tell why.
2. What was the attitude of the poet toward her subject? Look back
   at the details in the poem and the figures of speech used to
   describe them.
3. How do you interpret the last two sentences of the poem, beginning with line 65?
4. Point out several examples of the way the short lines intensify
   the succession of images.

The Express

STEPHEN SPENDER

After the first powerful plain manifesto
The black statement of pistons, without more fuss
But gliding like a queen, she leaves the station.
Without bowing and with restrained unconcern
She passes the houses which humbly crowd outside,   5
The gasworks, and at last the heavy page
Of death, printed by gravestones in the cemetery.
Beyond the town there lies the open country
Where, gathering speed, she acquires mystery,
The luminous self-possession of ships on ocean.   10
It is now she begins to sing—at first quite low
Then loud, and at last with a jazzy madness—
The song of her whistle screaming at curves,
Of deafening tunnels, brakes, innumerable bolts.
And always light, aerial, underneath   15
Goes the elate meter of her wheels.
Steaming through metal landscape on her lines
She plunges new eras of wild happiness
Where speed throws up strange shapes, broad curves
And parallels clean like the steel of guns.   20
At last, further than Edinburgh or Rome,
Beyond the crest of the world, she reaches night
Where only a low streamline brightness
Of phosphorus on the tossing hills is white.
Ah, like a comet through flames, she moves entranced   25
Wrapt in her music no bird song, no, nor bough
Breaking with honey buds, shall ever equal.

1. Make a list of the vivid images in this poem. To which senses do they appeal?
2. What is a *manifesto?* How does it apply to the train?
3. "Gliding like a queen," is a direct comparison (simile) between unlike things. Find another example of a simile in the poem.
4. The train is called *she* throughout the poem. This figurative use of language is called *personification,* because it endows inanimate objects with human qualities. With what qualities is the express train endowed?

I Like to See It Lap the Miles

EMILY DICKINSON

I like to see it lap the miles,
And lick the valleys up,
And stop to feed itself at tanks;
And then, prodigious, step

Around a pile of mountains,   5
And, supercilious, peer
In shanties by the sides of roads;
And then a quarry pare

To fit its sides, and crawl between,
Complaining all the while   10
In horrid, hooting stanza;
Then chase itself down hill

And neigh like Boanerges;
Then, punctual as a star,
Stop—docile and omnipotent—   15
At its own stable door.

1. At what point in the poem did you discover that two things are being compared? What are they? Is this an implied or a direct comparison?
2. The words *lap* and *lick* begin a succession of images, all of them related, most of them expressed in the verbs. Trace these images throughout the poem.
3. Look up the name *Boanerges* in a dictionary or encyclopedia. How appropriate is the name and the simile to the total picture created by the poem?
4. The rhythm is regular except in the last stanza. Point out the line which shows a change in rhythmical feet. What reason can you give for the change?
5. Describe the attitudes toward trains expressed by Stephen Spender and Emily Dickinson.

To Autumn

JOHN KEATS

Season of mists and mellow fruitfulness,
    Close bosom-friend of the maturing sun;
Conspiring with him how to load and bless
    With fruit the vines that round the thatch eaves run;
To bend with apples the mossed cottage-trees,   5
    And fill all fruit with ripeness to the core;
    To swell the gourd, and plump the hazel shells
With a sweet kernel; to set budding more,
    And still more, later flowers for the bees,
    Until they think warm days will never cease,   10
    For Summer has o'er-brimmed their clammy cells.

Who hath not seen thee oft amid thy store?
    Sometimes whoever seeks abroad may find

Thee sitting careless on a granary floor,
    Thy hair soft-lifted by the winnowing wind;   15
Or on a half-reaped furrow sound asleep,
    Drowsed with the fume of poppies, while thy hook
    Spares the next swath and all its twined flowers:
And sometime like a gleaner thou dost keep
    Steady thy laden head across a brook;   20
    Or by a cider-press, with patient look,
    Thou watchest the last oozings, hours by hours.

Where are the songs of Spring? Ay, where are they?
    Think not of them, thou hast thy music too,—
While barred clouds bloom the soft-dying day,   25
And touch the stubble-plains with rosy hue;
Then in a wailful choir the small gnats mourn
    Among the river sallows, ° borne aloft   willows
    Or sinking as the light wind lives or dies;
And full-grown lambs loud bleat from hilly bourn; °   country 30
    Hedge-crickets sing; and now with treble soft
    The redbreast whistles from a gardencroft;
    And gathering swallows twitter in the skies.

1. Point out the images that convey the richness of autumn.
2. In the second stanza autumn is personified by the word *thee*.
   Show how the imagery in stanza 2 develops the personification.
3. The poem is largely descriptive of autumn, but in the last stanza
   the poet has suggested an underlying message or meaning. What
   is it? Seek for it in the contrast set up between spring and autumn.
4. Study the repeated initial consonant sounds (alliteration), such
   as the *m* sound in the first two lines. Study also the effect of repeated vowel sounds (assonance). What sound effects are produced by onomatopoeia, single words like *winnowing* and *twitter*
   which imitate a natural sound?
5. Look at line 33. How do its rhythm and meaning give a sense of
   finality to the poem?

A Noiseless Patient Spider

WALT WHITMAN

A noiseless patient spider,
I mark'd where on a little promontory it stood isolated,
Mark'd how to explore the vacant vast surrounding,
It launch'd forth filament, filament, filament, out of itself,
Ever unreeling them, ever tirelessly speeding them.   5

And you O my soul where you stand,
Surrounded, detached, in measureless oceans of space,
Ceaselessly musing, venturing, throwing, seeking the spheres to
    connect them,
Till the bridge you will need be form'd, till the ductile anchor
    hold,
Till the gossamer thread you fling catch somewhere, O my
    soul.   10

1. What likenesses does the poet see between a spider and a man's
   soul? How does the spider explore his "vacant vast surrounding"?
   Can you suggest how the soul might explore its "oceans of space"?
   What is meant by "measureless oceans of space"?
2. What is the basic imagery that the poet builds up through the
   poem? In discussing this, first define *promontory*; then consider
   the poet's use of such words as *launched* and *unreeling*. What is
   the purpose of the first stanza of this poem?
3. The spider's goal is security and a good dinner. What is man's
   goal? What is his needed bridge? What is his anchor? Why is he
   seeking "the spheres to connect"?

On the Grasshopper
and the Cricket

JOHN KEATS

The poetry of earth is never dead:
  When all the birds are faint with the hot sun,
  And hide in cooling trees, a voice will run
From hedge to hedge about the new-mown mead;
That is the Grasshopper's—he takes the lead   5
  In summer luxury,—he has never done
  With his delights; for when tired out with fun
He rests at ease beneath some pleasant weed.
The poetry of earth is ceasing never:
  On a lone winter evening, when the frost   10
    Has wrought a silence, from the stove there shrills
The Cricket's song, in warmth increasing ever,
  And seems to one in drowsiness half lost,
    The Grasshopper's among some grassy hills.

1. What is the "poetry of earth"? Does the poet succeed in proving
   the statement he makes in line 1? Explain.
2. Show how the last six lines parallel the first eight.

The Chambered Nautilus

OLIVER WENDELL HOLMES

This is the ship of pearl, which, poets feign,°   pretend
    Sails the unshadowed main,—
    The venturous bark that flings
On the sweet summer wind its purpled wings
In gulfs enchanted, where the siren sings   5
    And coral reefs lie bare,
Where the cold sea-maids rise to sun their streaming hair.

Its webs of living gauze no more unfurl;
    Wrecked is the ship of pearl!
    And every chambered cell,   10
Where its dim dreaming life was wont to dwell,
As the frail tenant shaped his growing shell,
    Before thee lies revealed,—
Its irised ceiling rent,° its sunless crypt unsealed!   broken open

Year after year beheld the silent toil   15
    That spread his lustrous coil;
    Still, as the spiral grew,
He left the past year's dwelling for the new,
Stole with soft step its shining archway through,
    Built up its idle door,   20
Stretched in his last-found home, and knew the old no more.

Thanks for the heavenly message brought by thee,
    Child of the wandering sea,
    Cast from her lap, forlorn!

From thy dead lips a clearer note is born   25
Than ever Triton ° blew from wreathèd horn!   a sea god
    While on mine ear it rings
Through the deep caves of thought I hear a voice that sings:—

Build thee more stately mansions, O my soul,
    As the swift seasons roll!   30
    Leave thy low-vaulted past!
Let each new temple, nobler than the last,
Shut thee from heaven with a dome more vast,
    Till thou at length art free,
Leaving thine outgrown shell by life's unresting sea!   35

1. If possible, secure pictures of the nautilus. Knowing what this animal looks like will make the details of the figure of speech easier to understand.
2. What would lead poets to call the chambered nautilus "a ship of pearl"? Trace its growth and development—as described in the poem—and its final wreck upon the shore.
3. What "heavenly message" was brought by the shell? Explain carefully the metaphor in the last stanza. What comparison did the poet make between the soul of man and the chambered nautilus? Some people feel the poet should allow the reader to draw the moral, not state it. Do you agree or disagree? Why?
4. Compare this poem with "A Noiseless Patient Spider." Does it carry the same message, a similar message, or a different message? Which do you consider the better poem? Give reasons to support your choice.

City Evening

E. B. WHITE

The light that burned me up by day
Decides a little while to stay,
And writes a long and golden scrawl
In tree-leaf shadows on my wall.
The bulbous sun has spilled his fire,   5
Impaled upon a Jersey spire;
And hard day-objects of the street
Grow soft, in the long light, and sweet.
Noon's hot fortissimo still clings,
Muted in many murmurings;   10
And with the lingering light o'erspread
My thoughts are all new garmented.
Far down the block in yellow ease
Behind a row of gold-tipped trees
The "L," like some old dream, goes by   15
Betwixt the Avenue and sky.

1. What effect does the coming of evening have on the thoughts
   and feelings of the poet? Is the change from day to night swift
   or gradual?
2. How does the personification of light in the first four lines
   heighten the effect of the images? Find other examples of personification.
3. Point out the words and lines you find most interesting because of
   the judicious blending of sound and image.

in Just-

E. E. CUMMINGS

in Just-
spring   when the world is mud-
luscious the little
lame balloonman

whistles   far   and wee   5

and eddieandbill come
running from marbles and
piracies and it's
spring

when the world is puddle-wonderful   10

the queer
old balloonman whistles
far   and   wee
and bettyandisbel come dancing

from hop-scotch and jump-rope and   15

it's
spring
and
        the

            goat-footed   20

balloonMan   whistles
far
and
wee

1. Whose spring is the poet describing? The term "Just-spring" is
   a compact way of saying, "When spring has suddenly come" or
   "When spring is really here."
2. Account for the spaces between words in lines 5, 13, and 21-24.
   What suggestion is there in the arrangement to show the reader
   how to read the poem? Try reading it aloud. How is fast and slow
   rhythm indicated in this poem? Compare lines 6–10 and lines
   16–24.
3. Why is the "balloonman" called "goat-footed"? Look up the god
   Pan in a dictionary or encyclopedia. Why is the allusion to Pan
   appropriate to the season?

The Warning

ADELAIDE CRAPSEY

Just now,
Out of the strange
Still dusk ... as strange, as still ...
A white moth flew. Why am I grown
So cold?   5

1. What is "the warning"? What is the single image in the poem
   that conveys the idea of "the warning"? Tell why you feel it is,
   or is not, an effective image.

That Bright Chimeric Beast

COUNTEE CULLEN

That bright chimeric beast
Conceived yet never born
Save in the poet's breast,
The white-flanked unicorn,
Never may be shaken   5
From his solitude;
Never may be taken
In any earthly wood.

That bird forever feathered,
Of its new self the sire,   10
After aeons weathered,
Reincarnate by fire,
Falcon may not nor eagle
Swerve from his eyrie,
Nor any crumb inveigle   15
Down to an earthly tree.

That fish of the dread regime
Invented to become
The fable and the dream
Of the Lord's aquarium,   20
Leviathan, the jointed
Harpoon was never wrought
By which the Lord's anointed
Will suffer to be caught.

Bird of the deathless breast, 25
Fish of the frantic fin,
That bright chimeric beast
Flashing the argent skin,—
If beasts like these you'd harry,
Plumb then the poet's dream; 30
Make it your aviary,
Make it your wood and stream.

There only shall the swish
Be heard of the regal fish;
There like a golden knife 35
Dart the feet of the unicorn,
And there, death brought to life,
The dead bird be reborn.

1. In the first three stanzas, the poet alludes to three legendary beasts—the unicorn, the phoenix, and the leviathan—and describes them briefly. To understand better the aptness of his descriptions, look up the word *chimeric* in a good dictionary and references to the three beasts in an encyclopedia. Why cannot these beasts be hunted by ordinary men using ordinary weapons?
2. What type of person would be interested in pursuing these beasts? Consider, now, whether the poet means specifically the unicorn, the phoenix, and the leviathan, or whether he means something larger, which can be represented by these three. Can they be found in the real or literal world? What kind of world do they inhabit? According to the poet, where must the man who seeks these beasts as prey go to pursue them? What does poetry offer the man who would make it his aviary, wood, and stream? What comment is the poet making on the role of poetry, the power of the imagination, and the world of the poet?

Driftwood

R. STANLEY PETERSON

Some wood is straight,
Clear-grained, with scarce
A knot to mar the texture.
Close-grown, it reached
Tall in the forest. Other   5
Wood is more tortured.
Standing on a promontory,
It took the wind and wave,
Its body fiber twisted
And filled itself with faults   10
Where limb droppings fell.
Flotsam planks and jetsom
Staves are thrown to fire,
But driftwood comes a prize
To the collector. He cherishes   15
Well the storm-tossed, bent,
The intricate rich carvings
Time presses on mortal things.

1. Why is driftwood the prize of the collector? What qualities does
   it possess that the "clear-grained" wood lacks?
2. The poet is describing a happening in nature; how could his observations be extended to an interpretation of life? What might
   the driftwood symbolize? What might the "clear-grained" wood
   symbolize? The poet seems to value the driftwood and, by implication, that which it symbolizes. Do you agree with him? Give
   reasons to support your opinion.

Spring

EDNA ST. VINCENT MILLAY

To what purpose, April, do you return again?
Beauty is not enough.
You can no longer quiet me with the redness
Of little leaves opening stickily.
I know what I know.   5
The sun is hot on my neck as I observe
The spikes of the crocus.
The smell of the earth is good.
It is apparent that there is no death.
But what does that signify?   10
Not only under ground are the brains of men
Eaten by maggots.
Life in itself
Is nothing,
An empty cup, a flight of uncarpeted stairs.   15
It is not enough that yearly, down this hill,
April
Comes like an idiot, babbling and strewing flowers.

1. Why does the return of April bring the poet no comfort? What
   attitude is revealed in line 10?
2. Explain the meaning of the metaphors in lines 11–15. Are they
   a contradiction of what was said earlier, or a development? Explain.
3. Identify the simile in lines 17–18. Why does the coming of April
   remind the poet of "an idiot"?
4. Note the repetition of *enough* in lines 2 and 16. What clues indicate what might be enough? Do you think she knows?

The Beautiful Changes

RICHARD WILBUR

One wading a Fall meadow finds on all sides
The Queen Anne's Lace lying like lilies
On water; it glides
So from the walker, it turns
Dry grass to a lake, as the slightest shade of you　　　　5
Valleys my mind in fabulous blue Lucernes.[1]

The beautiful changes as a forest is changed
By a chameleon's tuning his skin to it;
As a mantis, arranged
On a green leaf, grows　　　　10
Into it, makes the leaf leafier, and proves
Any greenness is deeper than anyone knows.

Your hands hold roses always in a way that says
They are not only yours; the beautiful changes
In such kind ways,　　　　15
Wishing ever to sunder
Things and things' selves for a second finding, to lose
For a moment all that it touches back to wonder.

[1] *Lucernes*, reference to Lake of Lucerne, Switzerland

1. The speaker in this poem attempts to describe how the "beautiful" (that is, that which is beautiful) changes and why it changes. Look again at stanza 1. What was the speaker doing? How was he able to make the already satisfying experience even more rewarding? What happened to make the beautiful change for him?

2. In stanza 2, special kinds of relationships are described. Why should the forest become more beautiful because of the action of the chameleon? Why should the leaf become "leafier" because a mantis apparently grows into it? What happens to make the "beautiful" change?

3. The "you" of stanza 1 is reintroduced in stanza 3. Who might the "you" be? What, in the tone the speaker uses in speaking of the "you," helps to give you some idea of the feeling he has for this person? How does this person make the beautiful change? Might there be something in the relationship between the speaker and the person that contributes to the change?

4. In stanza 3, the speaker tells why the beautiful changes. What reason does he give? What might a "second finding" be? How might this "second finding" be connected to the way the speaker perceived the meadow and the forest? What does a viewer gain when the "beautiful" loses "all that it touches back to wonder"?

Sea Lullaby

ELINOR WYLIE

The old moon is tarnished
With smoke of the flood,
The dead leaves are varnished
With color like blood,

A treacherous smiler   5
With teeth white as milk,
A savage beguiler
In sheathings of silk,

The sea creeps to pillage,
She leaps on her prey;   10
A child of the village
Was murdered today.

She came up to meet him
In a smooth golden cloak,
She choked him and beat him   15
To death, for a joke.

Her bright locks were tangled,
She shouted for joy,
With one hand she strangled
A strong little boy.   20

Now in silence she lingers
Beside him all night
To wash her long fingers
In silvery light.

FORM
AND STRUCTURE
IN POETRY

Form and Structure in Poetry

An understanding of poetry may begin with the pleasure of hearing or reading a well-told story or of sharing the enthusiasm of the poet. It may grow out of an increased power to appreciate the image, the figure of speech, or the symbol. It may result from an intellectual identification with the poet's meaning or intention. No matter how or when it began, it can never be complete until the reader has acquired a knowledge and appreciation of the particular forms and structures that distinguish poetry from other works of literature.

In some works of art, the plan behind the work is fairly easy to see. The form and structure are clear. This is true of a Greek temple, a Mozart sonata, or a folk ballad. It is not true of an ornate cathedral, a modern symphony, or the revolutionary poems of E. E. Cummings. Yet there is a plan behind each work; each has a form and a discipline. The reader of poetry, as well as the student of music or of architecture, has a responsibility to discover the basic form of the work and the discipline. He must try to see why the artist chose that form rather than another to embody the substance of his idea and the spirit of his enthusiasm. He must try to understand the discipline involved in the creation of the work.

There are any number of forms and structures in poetry. It is not possible to learn everything about all of them; it is possible, however, to understand that each poem has a form, and that, for each good poem, it is the best form. It is also possible to examine each poem, to find its structure, and to see how this structure *is* the poem as much as the language is the poem.

Poets are free to make a wide variety of choices as they search for the right form to express the statement they wish to make. Some may choose the restricted sonnet or some tight rhyme scheme; others may choose a looser, unrhymed structure, with lines of uneven length. There are a number of choices available, but usually only one is the best.

The choice of form is sometimes determined by the poetic conventions of the time. During the Elizabethan period, poets favored the sonnet and playwrights wrote their dialogue in blank verse. The eighteenth century writers shared a preference for the couplet. None of these forms satisfied early twentieth century poets, who used a more versatile form called *free verse*. The poet today shares this enthusiasm for free verse, but he recognizes and frequently employs what he finds useful in previously popular forms. In his choice and arrangement of words he sometimes makes a greater appeal to the reader's eye than to his ear.

The poems in this section will introduce you to a wide variety of stanza forms and verse patterns. As you read each poem and, with the help of the questions, analyze its form and meaning, seek for the skeleton or structure around which the poem is built. Also try to discover why the form which the poet chose was best suited to the idea and feeling he wanted to express. Often the relationship between the form and structure of a poem and its total meaning is elusive, but it is there for the careful and appreciative reader to discover.

Loveliest of Trees

A. E. HOUSMAN

Loveliest of trees, the cherry now
Is hung with bloom along the bough,
And stands about the woodland ride °   (riding), a district in
Wearing white for Eastertide.   England established for
                                         taxing purposes

Now, of my threescore years and ten,   5
Twenty will not come again,
And take from seventy springs a score,
It only leaves me fifty more.

And since to look at things in bloom
Fifty springs are little room,   10
About the woodland I will go
To see the cherry hung with snow.

1. What reason does the poet give for going to see "the cherry hung with snow"?
2. The four-line stanza is the most common one in English poetry. In it, the poet can achieve simplicity or complexity by varying the length of line, changing the rhyme scheme and rhythm pattern, and introducing refrain lines.
3. The predominant rhythm in this poem is established in the second line, "Is hung with bloom along the bough." Because there are four iambic feet in this line, it is called *iambic tetrameter* (the Greek-derived word meaning "four measures or feet").
4. Compare the rhythms in the first two lines of the first stanza, of the second stanza, of the third. What parallels might someone see among these changing rhythms, the change in seasons of the year, and the changes in one's life as he grows older?

Sir Patrick Spens

ANONYMOUS

The king sits in Dumferling toune,
 Drinking the blude-reid wine:
"O whar will I get a guid sailor,
 To sail this schip of mine?"

Up and spak an eldern knicht,   5
 Sat at the king's richt kne:
"Sir Patrick Spens is the best sailor
 That sails upon the se."

The king has written a braid ° letter,   official
 And signed it wi' his hand,   10
And sent it to Sir Patrick Spens,
 Was walking on the sand.

The first line that Sir Patrick red,
 A loud laugh laughed he;
The next line that Sir Patrick red,   15
 The teir blinded his ee.

"O wha is this has don this deid,
 This ill deid don to me,
To send me out this time o' the yeir,
 To sail upon the se?   20

"Mak hast, mak hast, my mirry men all,
 Our guid schip sails the morne:"
"O say na sae,° my master deir,   so
 For I feir a deadlie storme.

"Late late yestreen I saw the new moone   25
    Wi' the auld moone in hir arme,
And I feir, I feir, my deir master,
    That we will cum to harme."

O our Scots nobles were richt laith °   reluctant
    To weet ° their cork-heild schoone; °   wet; shoes 30
Bot lang owre a' the play wer playd,
    Thair hats they swam aboone.°   on the water

O lang, lang, may their ladies sit,
    Wi' thair fans into their hand,
Or eir they se Sir Patrick Spens   35
    Cum sailing to the land.

O lang, lang, may the ladies stand,
    Wi' thair gold kembs ° in their hair,   combs
Waiting for their ain deir lords,
    For they'll see thame na mair.   40

Have ° owre, have owre to Aberdour,   half
    It's fiftie fadom deip,
And thair lies guid Sir Patrick Spens,
    Wi' the Scots lords at his feit.

1. When examining the form of a folk ballad, you must be aware
   that ballads were meant to be sung and that often they were
   passed on orally—for that strongly influenced their form. Why
   would a four-line stanza be appropriate? Why would a poet make
   use of a definite rhyme scheme and rhythm pattern? Identify the
   rhyme scheme and rhythm in the first stanza.
2. What similarities do you find in the way this ballad is told as
   compared with other folk ballads in the first section (pages 4–10)?
   What, in general, seem to be the characteristics that folk ballads
   have in common?

How Doth the Little Crocodile

LEWIS CARROLL

How doth the little crocodile
   Improve his shining tail,
And pour the waters of the Nile
   On every shining scale!

How cheerfully he seems to grin,   5
   How neatly spreads his claws,
And welcomes little fishes in
   With gently smiling jaws!
     —from *Alice in Wonderland*

1. Is the rhythmic pattern here regular or irregular? Why do you suppose the writer chose such a pattern?
2. Is the poem finally childish or mature? Explain your answer.

The Schoolmaster

OLIVER GOLDSMITH

Beside yon straggling fence that skirts the way,
With blossomed furze unprofitably gay—
There, in his noisy mansion, skilled to rule,
The village master taught his little school.
A man severe he was, and stern to view;   5
I knew him well, and every truant knew;
Well had the boding° tremblers learned to trace   watchful
The day's disasters in his morning face;
Full well they laughed with counterfeited glee
At all his jokes, for many a joke had he;   10
Full well the busy whisper, circling round,
Conveyed the dismal tidings when he frowned.
Yet he was kind, or if severe in aught,
The love he bore to learning was in fault. . . .

1. What opinion did you form of the schoolmaster? Explain.
2. Note that this poem is written in couplet form: the lines rhyme in pairs. Note, too, that many of the pairs of rhymed lines contain a complete thought. Such lines are called closed couplets. This form was commonly used in the eighteenth century.
3. Do all of the lines contain the same number of accented syllables? What is the predominant meter? Point out and identify variations of this meter. What virtues do you see in the use of the couplet?
4. Now read "Endymion" (on the next page) which is also written in couplet form. Note, however, that now the couplets become "open" rather than "closed." To complete the sense, the reader must read more than the two rhymed lines.

5. Note the number of pauses which Keats indicates within the lines. Where do they occur? What do they contribute to the poem?
6. "Proem" is rich in imagery. Point out examples you particularly liked. Also point out the relationship between the statement in line 1 and the statement in lines 11–13.
7. What is the "endless fountain"? Why is it immortal?

Proem from Endymion

JOHN KEATS

A thing of beauty is a joy forever:
Its loveliness increases; it will never
Pass into nothingness; but still will keep
A bower quiet for us, and a sleep
Full of sweet dreams, and health, and quiet breathing.   5
Therefore, on every morrow, are we wreathing
A flowery band to bind us to the earth,
Spite of despondence, of the inhuman dearth
Of noble natures, of the gloomy days,
Of all the unhealthy and o'er-darkened ways   10
Made for our searching: yes, in spite of all,
Some shape of beauty moves away the pall
From our dark spirits. Such the sun, the moon,
Trees old, and young, sprouting a shady boon
For simple sheep; and such are daffodils   15
With the green world they live in; and clear rills
That for themselves a cooling covert make
'Gainst the hot season; the mid-forest brake,°   ferns
Rich with a sprinkling of fair musk-rose blooms:
And such too is the grandeur of the dooms°   destinies 20
We have imagined for the mighty dead;

All lovely tales that we have heard or read:
An endless fountain of immortal drink,
Pouring unto us from the heaven's brink.

Nightmare

W. S. GILBERT

When you're lying awake with a dismal headache, and repose is
    taboo'd by anxiety,
I conceive you may use any language you choose to indulge in,
    without impropriety;
For your brain is on fire—the bedclothes conspire of usual slum-
    ber to plunder you:
First your counterpane goes, and uncovers your toes, and your
    sheet slips demurely from under you;
Then the blanketing tickles—you feel like mixed pickles, so
    terribly sharp is the pricking,   5
And you're hot, and you're cross, and you tumble and toss till
    there's nothing 'twixt you and the ticking.
Then the bedclothes all creep to the ground in a heap, and you
    pick 'em all up in a tangle;
Next your pillow resigns and politely declines to remain at its
    usual angle!
Well, you get some repose in the form of a doze, with hot eye-
    balls and head ever aching.
But your slumbering teems with such horrible dreams that you'd
    very much better be waking. . . .   10
You're a regular wreck, with a crick in your neck, and no wonder
    you snore, for your head's on the floor, and you've needles
    and pins from your soles to your shins, and your flesh is

a-creep; for your left leg's asleep, and you've cramp in your
   toes, and a fly on your nose, and some fluff in your lung, and
   a feverish tongue, and a thirst that's intense, and a general
   sense that you haven't been sleeping in clover;
But the darkness has passed, and it's daylight at last, and the
   night has been long—ditto ditto my song—and thank goodness they're both of them over!

—from Iolanthe

1. Does the title refer to a bad dream or to an experience? Explain.
2. What elements contribute to the humor of this poem?
3. Note that couplets are used in this poem as well as in those by
   Goldsmith and Keats. Account for the different effects achieved
   in each.

We Never Know How High

EMILY DICKINSON

We never know how high we are
   Till we are called to rise;
And then, if we are true to plan,
   Our statures touch the skies.

The heroism we recite   5
   Would be a daily thing,
Did not ourselves the cubits warp
   For fear to be a king.

The Dark Hills

EDWIN ARLINGTON ROBINSON

Dark hills at evening in the west,
Where sunset hovers like a sound
Of golden horns that sang to rest
Old bones of warriors under ground,
Far now from all the bannered ways 5
Where flash the legions of the sun,
You fade—as if the last of days
Were fading and all wars were done.

1. The poet has made his poem of one sentence. Read the poem aloud. Chart the rhythm and rhyme schemes. How does the poet on the one hand make use of a very regular pattern and on the other manage to make it unobtrusive?
2. How does the poet prepare us for the statement in lines 7–8? Connotations of words are the associations they call to mind when we read or hear them. Consider the connotations of key words in lines 3–6 as you formulate your answer to this question.
3. What is the literal statement of the poem? What might be its larger meaning?

Interlude 3

KARL SHAPIRO

Writing, I crushed an insect with my nail
And thought nothing at all. A bit of wing
Caught my eye then, a gossamer so frail

And exquisite, I saw in it a thing
That scorned the grossness of the thing I wrote.   5
It hung upon my finger like a sting.

A leg I noticed next, fine as a mote,
"And on this frail eyelash he walked," I said,
"And climbed and walked like any mountain-goat."

And in this mood I sought the little head,   10
But it was lost; then in my heart a fear
Cried out, "A life—why beautiful, why dead!"

It was a mite that held itself most dear,
So small I could have drowned it with a tear.

1. Why did his experience make such a deep impression on the poet?
   As he thought over what had happened, why did he feel fear?
   What universal concern does he suggest in line 12?
2. This three-line stanza is called *terza rima,* a form used by Dante
   in his *Divine Comedy.* Its rhyme is linked. Look back at the poem
   and describe how it is linked. What is the predominant rhythm in
   the poem?

When I Was One-and-Twenty

A. E. HOUSMAN

When I was one-and-twenty
   I heard a wise man say,
"Give crowns and pounds and guineas
   But not your heart away;
Give pearls away and rubies   5
   But keep your fancy free."
But I was one-and-twenty,
   No use to talk to me.

When I was one-and-twenty
   I heard him say again,   10
"The heart out of the bosom
   Was never given in vain;
'Tis paid with sighs a-plenty
   And sold for endless rue."
And I am two-and-twenty,   15
   And oh, 'tis true, 'tis true.

1. When we speak of the *tone* of a poem, we refer to the way the speaker in the poem seems to feel about the experience being described—his attitude. How would you describe the tone of the first fourteen lines of this poem? Which two lines express that tone most clearly?
2. Where does the tone suddenly change? In your answer, consider the way the second stanza seems to develop as compared with the first. How did the poet's form and structure serve to make this change particularly effective?

Break, Break, Break

ALFRED, LORD TENNYSON

Break, break, break,
   On thy cold grey stones, O Sea!
And I would that my tongue could utter
   The thoughts that arise in me.

O well for the fisherman's boy,   5
   That he shouts with his sister at play!
O well for the sailor lad,
   That he sings in his boat on the bay!

And the stately ships go on
   To their haven under the hill;   10
But O for the touch of a vanished hand,
   And the sound of a voice that is still!

Break, break, break,
   At the foot of thy crags, O Sea!
But the tender grace of a day that is dead   15
   Will never come back to me.

1. What is the poet mourning? What corresponds to his mood; what is in contrast to it? How do lines 1 and 13 emphasize the sorrowful mood? What is the effect of the pauses after each spondaic foot?
2. Chart the rhythm of this poem. All but lines 1 and 13 contain at least one anapestic foot or triple movement. How does the rhythm support the meaning of the poem?
3. Read this poem aloud, noting the alliteration and assonance. Only then will you experience its full effect.

Sonnet 30

WILLIAM SHAKESPEARE

When to the sessions of sweet silent thought
I summon up remembrance of things past,
I sigh the lack of many a thing I sought,
And with old woes new wail my dear time's waste.
Then can I drown an eye, unused to flow,   5
For precious friends hid in death's dateless night,
And weep afresh love's long since canceled woe,
And moan the expense of many a vanished sight.
Then can I grieve at grievances foregone,
And heavily from woe to woe tell o'er   10
The sad account of fore-bemoanèd moan,
Which I new pay as if not paid before.
    But if the while I think on thee, dear friend,
    All losses are restored and sorrows end.

1. This poem is written in sonnet form, a favorite form with Italian poets and one that was widely copied by English poets during the sixteenth and seventeenth centuries. The English retained the fourteen-line stanza but many poets used an organization different from the Italian (the Italian sonnet is described on page 103). The English sonnet, which is often called the Shakespearean sonnet, is made up of three quatrains and a concluding couplet. The rhyme scheme follows this pattern:

   abab cdcd efef gg

   The predominant rhythm is iambic pentameter: five iambic feet to each line.

2. From the rhyme scheme you can easily see the organization of the sonnet and the way the thought is developed. State the over-all idea or theme expressed in the first quatrain. Show how it is developed in the second and third quatrains. What purpose is served by the couplet, lines 13 and 14?

3. Is the couplet in this sonnet *opened* or *closed*? Explain. Where else have you seen such a couplet used?

4. There are two instances of imperfect rhyme: end words which do not quite match in sound. Point these out.

5. It is not easy to express one's thoughts and feelings exactly in fourteen lines and within the other restrictions of the sonnet form. Can you think of any advantages that the sonnet form offers for the expression of such ideas and emotions as those in this poem? Analyze the development of the ideas in this poem in order to formulate your answer.

Composed upon *Westminster Bridge*

WILLIAM WORDSWORTH

Earth has not anything to show more fair:
Dull would he be of soul who could pass by
A sight so touching in its majesty:
This City now doth like a garment wear
The beauty of the morning; silent, bare,   5
Ships, towers, domes, theaters and temples lie
Open unto the fields, and to the sky;
All bright and glittering in the smokeless air.
Never did sun more beautifully steep
In his first splendor, valley, rock, or hill;   10
Ne'er saw I, never felt, a calm so deep!
The river glideth at his own sweet will:
Dear God! the very houses seem asleep;
And all that mighty heart is lying still!

1. What is the over-all idea or theme of this sonnet?
2. Instead of using the English form for this sonnet, Wordsworth
   used the Italian form, which has a somewhat different organization. In the first eight lines—the *octave*—he states and develops
   the theme. In the last six lines—the *sestet*—he presents the conclusion. Note the absence of the final couplet. Usually the rhyme
   scheme follows this pattern:

   abba abba cde cde

   How closely does Wordsworth follow this rhyme scheme? Where
   do the variations occur?

3. The octave usually sets the scene, states the theme, describes the action, or narrates an incident. The sestet makes the application, draws the conclusion, or states the poet's philosophy. Examine this sonnet. What is presented in the octave? In the sestet? What is the meaning of the last line?

The Soldier

RUPERT BROOKE

If I should die, think only this of me:
    That there's some corner of a foreign field
That is forever England. There shall be
    In that rich earth a richer dust concealed;
A dust whom England bore, shaped, made aware,   5
    Gave, once, her flowers to love, her ways to roam,
A body of England's, breathing English air,
    Washed by the rivers, blest by suns of home.

And think, this heart, all evil shed away,
    A pulse in the eternal mind, no less   10
        Gives somewhere back the thoughts by England given;
Her sights and sound; dreams happy as her day;
    And laughter, learnt of friends; and gentleness,
        In hearts at peace, under an English heaven.

1. The theme of this sonnet is both patriotic and philosophical. Explain why. Discuss the statement of the octave and of the sestet.
2. What rhyme scheme does the poet use? Show how this sonnet is a combination of the Italian form and the English form.

from *Julius Caesar*

WILLIAM SHAKESPEARE

Antony. O, pardon me, thou bleeding piece of earth,
That I am meek and gentle with these butchers!
Thou art the ruins of the noblest man
That ever lived in the tide of times.
Woe to the hand that shed this costly blood!   5
Over thy wounds now do I prophesy,
Which like dumb mouths do ope their ruby lips
To beg the voice and utterance of my tongue,
A curse shall light upon the limbs of men;
Domestic fury and fierce civil strife   10
Shall cumber all the parts of Italy;
Blood and destruction shall be so in use,
And dreadful objects so familiar,
That mothers shall but smile when they behold
Their infants quarter'd with the hands of war;   15
All pity chok'd with custom of fell deeds:
And Caesar's spirit ranging for revenge,
With Ate° by his side come hot from hell,   *Greek goddess*
Shall in these confines with a monarch's   *personifying the*
    voice   *divine punishment*
                                               for crimes committed
Cry 'Havoc,' and let slip the dogs of war;   20
That this foul deed shall smell above the earth
With carrion men, groaning for burial.

1. In this speech Antony is addressing his friend Caesar, who has
   been murdered by the conspirators. They have left him alone with
   the body, and this statement follows their departure.

2. Study the figures of speech, the vivid imagery of this passage. What gives this passage its great strength?
3. Shakespeare wrote his plays in *blank verse:* unrhymed iambic pentameter (five iambic feet to the line). It achieved its highest development in Shakespeare's use of it. Give reasons why it is so well suited to dramatic literature.
4. The predominant rhythm is iambic pentameter, but Shakespeare departs from this rhythm when sense and dramatic effect require. Chart the metrical pattern of this piece and point out any variations. Account for these variations.

"*Out, Out —* "

ROBERT FROST

The buzz-saw snarled and rattled in the yard
And made dust and dropped stove-length sticks of wood,
Sweet-scented stuff when the breeze drew across it.
And from there those that lifted eyes could count
Five mountain ranges one behind the other   5
Under the sunset far into Vermont.
And the saw snarled and rattled, snarled and rattled,
As it ran light, or had to bear a load.
And nothing happened: day was all but done.
Call it a day, I wish they might have said   10
To please the boy by giving him the half hour
That a boy counts so much when saved from work.
His sister stood beside them in her apron
To tell them 'Supper.' At the word, the saw,
As if to prove saws knew what supper meant,   15
Leaped out at the boy's hand, or seemed to leap—
He must have given the hand. However it was,
Neither refused the meeting. But the hand!

The boy's first outcry was a rueful laugh,
As he swung toward them holding up his hand   20
Half in appeal, but half as if to keep
The life from spilling. Then the boy saw all—
Since he was old enough to know, big boy
Doing a man's work, though a child at heart—
He saw all spoiled. 'Don't let him cut my hand off—   25
The doctor, when he comes. Don't let him, sister!'
So. But the hand was gone already.
The doctor put him in the dark of ether.
He lay and puffed his lips out with his breath.
And then—the watcher at his pulse took fright.   30
No one believed. They listened at his heart.
Little—less—nothing!—and that ended it.
No more to build on there. And they, since they
Were not the one dead, turned to their affairs.

1. The title of this poem is taken from a famous speech in *Macbeth* beginning "Out, out, brief candle . . ." in which the "brief candle" is a metaphor for life. Why is the title appropriate to the content of this poem?
2. What is the predominant rhythm in this poem? Is it similar to or different from Shakespeare's rhythm in Antony's speech?
3. Comment on Robert Frost's language in this poem as compared with Shakespeare's language. What differences do you observe? In what ways does Frost's language seem appropriate or inappropriate in this poem?
4. "To keep the life from spilling" is a figure of speech called *metonymy*. In this figure of speech, the name of one thing is used in place of another that is closely associated with it. ("The White House has decided," for example, means that the President has decided.) In this metonymy, life is used in place of what?

Winter Trees

WILLIAM CARLOS WILLIAMS

All the complicated details
of the attiring and
the disattiring are completed!
A liquid moon
moves gently among   5
the long branches.
Thus having prepared their buds
against a sure winter,
the wise trees
stand sleeping in the cold.   10

1. If you were to hear this free verse poem read, would you be certain
   that it was a poem? The lines do not rhyme, nor do they have a
   predominant rhythm. It is almost necessary to see it in print to
   know it is a poem. The arrangement of the lines in a free verse
   poem is particularly important. Each line is as it is so that you can
   read the poem just as the poet intended it to be read.
2. Line 1 is the subject of a sentence. What does the poet force you
   to do by positioning it by itself in one line? What greater emphasis is given to line 3 because the *and* in line 2 has been left hang-
   ing? What is the effect of having "A liquid moon" separated from
   its predicate "moves . . ."? Why is it appropriate for the preposi-
   tion *among* to be separated from its object? Show how the meaning of the poem is supported by the arrangement of the lines.
3. What is the mood of this poem? How do the images contribute to
   the mood? Which words are especially appropriate? What image
   do you find most effective?

Cavalry Crossing a Ford

WALT WHITMAN

A line in long array where they wind betwixt green islands,
They take a serpentine course, their arms flash in the sun—hark
    to the musical clank,
Behold the silvery river, in it the splashing horses loitering stop
    to drink,
Behold the brown-faced men, each group, each person, a picture,
    the negligent rest on the saddles,
Some emerge on the opposite bank, others are just entering the
    ford—while,   5
Scarlet and blue and snowy white,
The guidon° flags flutter gayly in the wind.   pennant, signal

1. Like "Song of the Open Road" (page 40), this Whitman poem is
   in free verse. Examine lines 1–5, line by line. What are you told
   in line 1? How are the images in lines 2–5 related to that of line 1?
   What is the effect of positioning —*while*, with its special punctuation at the end of line 5? What is the effect of line 6, which mentions only colors? What is finally accomplished by line 7?
2. There are many sensory impressions in this poem. What images
   appeal to the eye? to the ear? to your sense of movement? Describe the atmosphere of the poem, using details from it to support your answer.

plato told

E. E. CUMMINGS

plato told

him:he couldn't
believe it(jesus

told him;he
wouldn't believe   5
it)lao

tsze
certainly told
him,and general
(yes   10

mam)
sherman;
and even
(believe it
or   15

not)you
told him:i told
him;we told him
(he didn't believe it,no

sir)it took 20
a nipponized bit of
the old sixth

avenue
el;in the top of his head:to tell

him 25

1. Cummings is one of the most extreme of modern poets. What purpose does he have in omitting capitals, breaking up lines, separating words, and introducing strange side comments?
2. How would you describe the structure of this poem? How does it grow in power? Why is there no punctuation after the last word, *him*?
3. You will need to know that scrap metal from the elevated tracks in New York was sold to Japan before their attack on Pearl Harbor.
4. Lao Tsze was a Chinese philosopher. What was it that Lao, Plato, and the others "told him"?

A Pact

EZRA POUND

I make a pact with you, Walt Whitman—
I have detested you long enough.
I come to you as a grown child
Who has had a pig-headed father;
I am old enough now to make friends.   5
It was you that broke the new wood,
Now is a time for carving.
We have one sap and one root—
Let there be commerce between us.

1. Describe the tone of this poem. Consider, for example, the effect of Pound's addressing Whitman by his full name. What is the effect of the last line on the tone of the poem?
2. What reasons does Pound give for finally making contact with Whitman? Explain lines 3-5. What is the meaning of *commerce* in this poem?
3. How does the form of the poem support its statement?

THE POEM
AS
IDEA

The Poem as Idea

All art has meaning. The painting, the symphony, the poem—
each expresses an idea in the mind of the creator. Therefore,
you may well ask of any work of art, "What does it mean? What
is the person who created it saying"?

The idea of a poem may be expressed in almost any form—
that which gives shape and meaning to the idea—and in any
pattern of sounds and rhythms. It may be presented in a single
image or revealed through many images. The sounds and images
may delight you, but you must also discover the idea. When you
have finished reading a poem, you must be able to say, "This is
what the poet is saying. This is what the words mean. This is what
I believe the poet had in mind when he wrote the poem."

Through the poems in this section you will explore some of
the eternal questions that concern all men. What is the meaning
of liberty, happiness, fame, progress? How should a man meet
death? What makes him hate? Why is he afraid? The poet attempts to answer these questions for himself. He cannot answer
them for you, but he can share with you his thoughts and feelings.
As you read his poem, concentrate first on what he says and what
he means. When that is clear, look for a deeper meaning implied
by the imagery or symbols. Finally, ask yourself, "What does all
this have to do with me"?

Prayers of Steel

CARL SANDBURG

Lay me on an anvil, O God.
Beat me and hammer me into a crowbar.
Let me pry loose old walls.
Let me lift and loosen old foundations.

Lay me on an anvil, O God.   5
Beat me and hammer me into a steel spike.
Drive me into the girders that hold a skyscraper together.
Take red-hot rivets and fasten me into the central girders.
Let me be the great nail holding a skyscraper through blue nights
    into white stars

1. Explain each of these symbols used in the first stanza: the anvil,
   the crowbar, old walls, old foundations.
2. Explain the new symbols used in the second stanza: the steel
   spike, the girders, the skyscraper.
3. What do you make of "blue nights" and "white stars"?
4. What prayers are expressed here in figurative language?

I Never Saw a Moor

EMILY DICKINSON

I never saw a moor,
I never saw the sea;
Yet know I how the heather looks,
And what a wave must be.

I never spoke with God,   5
Nor visited in heaven;
Yet certain am I of the spot
As if the chart were given.

1. By what power is the speaker able to know what she has never
   seen?
2. What relationship is there between the idea expressed in stanza 1
   and that expressed in stanza 2?
3. Look again at Emily Dickinson's poem on page 96. What similarities do you find in such matters as style, structure, kinds of
   rhymes?

Abraham Lincoln Walks at Midnight

VACHEL LINDSAY

It is portentous, and a thing of state
That here at midnight, in our little town
A mourning figure walks, and will not rest,
Near the old courthouse pacing up and down,

Or by his homestead, or in shadowed yards   5
He lingers where his children used to play,
Or through the market, on the well-worn stones
He stalks until the dawn-stars burn away.

A bronzed, lank man! His suit of ancient black,
A famous high top hat and plain worn shawl   10
Make him the quaint great figure that men love,
The prairie lawyer, master of us all.

He cannot sleep upon his hillside now.
He is among us:—as in times before!
And we who toss and lie awake for long   15
Breathe deep, and start, to see him pass the door.

His head is bowed. He thinks on men and kings.
Yea, when the sick world cries, how can he sleep?
Too many peasants fight, they know not why,
Too many homesteads in black terror weep.   20

The sins of all the war lords burn his heart.
He sees the dreadnoughts scouring every main.
He carries on his shawl-wrapped shoulders now
The bitterness, the folly and the pain.

He cannot rest until a spirit-dawn   25
Shall come;—the shining hope of Europe free:
The league of sober folk, the Workers' Earth,
Bringing long peace to Cornland, Alp and Sea.

It breaks his heart that kings must murder still,
That all his hours of travail here for men   30
Seem yet in vain. And who will bring white peace
That he may sleep upon his hill again?

1. Why is it portentous that Lincoln "is among us:–as in times
   before"? What "spirit-dawn" must come before he can rest?
2. The references made in the poem are to World War I. Draw
   parallels between the world the poet is talking about and our
   present world. What improvements have been made in the "sick
   world" that might give some comfort? What conditions might
   make the "spirit-dawn" even more remote?
3. What lines describe Lincoln's attitude toward war? If peace
   comes, who would probably bring it? During his lifetime, how did
   he feel about men taking up arms against their fellow men?
4. What message is conveyed in this poem? Is the mood one of hope
   or despair? Which words convey the mood?

Solitude

ALEXANDER POPE

Happy the man, whose wish and care
A few paternal acres bound,
Content to breathe his native air
    In his own ground:

Whose herds with milk, whose fields with bread,   5
Whose flocks supply him with attire;
Whose trees in summer yield him shade,
    In winter fire:

Blest, who can unconcern'dly find
Hours, days, and years, slide soft away   10
In health of body, peace of mind,
    Quiet by day:

Sound sleep by night; study and ease
Together mixt, sweet recreation,
And innocence, which most does please   15
    With meditation.

Thus let me live, unseen, unknown;
Thus unlamented let me die;
Steal from the world, and not a stone
    Tell where I lie.   20

1. What kind of person would equate solitude with the happy life?
   How convincing is the poet's description of this life? In your
   opinion, what are its advantages and disadvantages?

2. Do you agree or disagree with the advice given in the last stanza? What joys and satisfactions would you miss if you lived unknown and died unlamented? What problems and heartaches would you be spared? Can happiness be found by avoiding the unpleasant? Explain.
3. Pope said of poetry: "What oft was thought but ne'er so well expressed." Is this expression of his idea in poetry more effective than a prose statement would be? Explain.

What Makes a Happy Life

MARCUS VALERIUS MARTIALIS

What makes a happy life, dear friend,
If thou wouldst briefly learn, attend—
An income left, not earned by toil;
Some acres of a kindly soil;
The pot unfailing on the fire;   5
No lawsuits, seldom town attire;
Health; strength with grace; a peaceful mind;
Shrewdness with honesty combined;
Plain living; equal friends and free;
Evenings of temperate gayety;   10
A wife discreet yet blithe and bright;
Sound slumber that lends wings to night.
With all thy heart embrace thy lot,
Wish not for death, and fear it not.
   —translated from the Latin by Goldwin Smith

1. How is the life described in this poem similar to, and different from, the life described in "Solitude"? Tell why you think it is, or is not, possible in today's world.
2. What kind of man would recommend the life described in this poem? Is it the kind of life that appeals to you? Explain.

To a Waterfowl

WILLIAM CULLEN BRYANT

Whither, midst falling dew,
While glow the heavens with the last steps of day,
Far, through their rosy depths, dost thou pursue
    Thy solitary way?

Vainly the fowler's ° eye   hunter's 5
Might mark thy distant flight to do thee wrong,
As, darkly seen against the crimson sky,
    Thy figure floats along.

Seek'st thou the plashy brink
Of weedy lake, or marge of river wide,   10
Or where the rocking billows rise and sink
    On the chafed ocean-side?

There is a Power whose care
Teaches thy way along that pathless coast—
The desert and illimitable air—   15
    Lone wandering, but not lost.

All day thy wings have fanned,
At that far height, the cold, thin atmosphere,
Yet stoop not, weary, to the welcome land,
    Though the dark night is near.   20

And soon that toil shall end;
Soon shalt thou find a summer home, and rest,
And scream among thy fellows; reeds shall bend,
    Soon, o'er thy sheltered nest.

Thou'rt gone, the abyss of heaven   25
Hath swallowed up thy form; yet, on my heart
Deeply has sunk the lesson thou hast given,
    And shall not soon depart.

He who, from zone to zone,
Guides through the boundless sky thy certain flight,   30
In the long way that I must tread alone,
    Will lead my steps aright.

1. At what line in the poem were you aware that the poet was
   developing a metaphor? What was he comparing? In what ways
   are they alike?
2. In stanzas 4 and 8, the poet refers to a Power that guides all
   living things. How are the ideas expressed in the two stanzas
   similar and different?
3. In this poem, as in "The Chambered Nautilus," the poet draws
   the moral for the reader. Would you have been able to infer it
   from the implied comparison? Would the poem have been more
   effective without the last stanza? Explain.
4. In the following poem, an idea is also conveyed through a metaphor. What is being compared? What is the poet saying?

Rust

MARY CAROLYN DAVIES

Iron, left in the rain
    And fog and dew,
With rust is covered. Pain
    Rusts into beauty too.

I know full well that this is so: 5
I had a heartbreak long ago.

Death, Be Not Proud

JOHN DONNE

Death, be not proud, though some have callèd thee
Mighty and dreadful, for thou art not so;
For those whom thou think'st thou dost overthrow
Die not, poor Death; nor yet canst thou kill me.
From rest and sleep, which but thy pictures be,   5
Much pleasure; then from thee much more must flow;
And soonest our best men with thee do go—
Rest of their bones and souls' delivery!
Thou'rt slave to fate, chance, kings, and desperate men,
And dost with poison, war, and sickness dwell;   10
And poppy or charms can make us sleep as well
And better than thy stroke. Why swell'st thou then?
One short sleep past, we wake eternally,
And Death shall be no more: Death, thou shalt die!

1. Why is Death called "poor"? Why is it unable to kill?
2. What comparison is made between rest, sleep, and death? What
   point is the poet trying to prove? How does he prove it? Complete this statement: If we get pleasure from rest and sleep,
   then....
3. How do you interpret lines 7 and 8? Is this thought consoling?
   Why?
4. The poet both addresses Death directly (the apostrophe) and
   personifies it. How do these poetic techniques intensify the
   dramatic effect of the poem and add to its emotional tone?
5. State in your own words the meaning of the last two lines. Has the
   poet convinced you that Death is neither mighty nor dreadful?

Crossing the Bar

ALFRED, LORD TENNYSON

Sunset and evening star,
   And one clear call for me!
And may there be no moaning of the bar,
   When I put out to sea,

But such a tide as moving seems asleep,   5
   Too full for sound and foam,
When that which drew from out the boundless deep
   Turns again home.

Twilight and evening bell,
   And after that the dark!   10
And may there be no sadness of farewell,
   When I embark;

For though from out our bourne ° of Time and   kingdom, land
   Place
   The flood may bear me far,
I hope to see my Pilot face to face   15
   When I have crossed the bar.

1. Compare the attitude toward Death expressed in this poem with
   the attitude expressed in "Death, Be Not Proud." Which of the
   two poems do you consider more effective? Why?
2. Trace the figure of speech that likens life and death to aspects
   of the sea. Explain the figurative meaning of *bar, sea, tide, sound
   and foam, boundless deep, home, twilight, evening bell, dark,
   embark, flood, Pilot.*

from *The Black Riders*

STEPHEN CRANE

A man saw a ball of gold in the sky;
He climbed for it,
And eventually he achieved it—
It was clay.

Now this is the strange part: 5
When the man went to the earth
And looked again,
Lo, there was the ball of gold.

Now this is the strange part:
It was a ball of gold.   10
Aye, by the heavens, it was a ball of gold.

1. Note the use of repetition in this poem. What is its effect? What
   is the effect of the repetition in lines 5 and 9?
2. What is the purpose of this poem? What statement is the poet
   making? In answering, consider the figurative meaning of *ball of
   gold, sky, clay*.
3. Retell this story, using as the protagonist a man living in your own
   times.

Ozymandias

PERCY BYSSHE SHELLEY

I met a traveler from an antique land
Who said: Two vast and trunkless legs of stone
Stand in the desert. Near them, on the sand,
Half sunk, a shattered visage lies, whose frown,
And wrinkled lip, and sneer of cold command,   5
Tell that its sculptor well those passions read
Which yet survive, stamped on these lifeless things,
The hand that mocked them and the heart that fed;
And on the pedestal these words appear:
"My name is Ozymandias, king of kings: 10
Look on my works, ye Mighty, and despair!"
Nothing beside remains. Round the decay
Of that colossal wreck, boundless and bare
The lone and level sands stretch far away.

1. What is ironic about the inscription on the pedestal? Describe the character of Ozymandias as revealed in this poem. What passions had the sculptor read?
2. In line 8, *hand* and *heart* are direct objects of the verb *survive*. Which refers to the sculptor? Which to the king? State in your own words the thought expressed in lines 3–8, beginning with "Near them, on the sand. . . ."
3. What is contrasted in the last three lines? How is the contrast made more dramatic by the sound of the words in lines 13 and 14?

The Hammers

RALPH HODGSON

Noise of hammers once I heard,
Many hammers, busy hammers,
Beating, shaping, night and day,
Shaping, beating dust and clay
To a palace; saw it reared;　　　　　　　　　　　5
Saw the hammers laid away.

And I listened, and I heard
Hammers beating, night and day,
In the palace newly reared,
Beating it to dust and clay:　　　　　　　　　　10
Other hammers, muffled hammers,
Silent hammers of decay.

1. Compare the beliefs expressed in this poem with those expressed
   in "Ozymandias." Do the poets share similar beliefs? Explain.
2. The symbol of the hammers has two possible meanings. Show
   how these two meanings are brought out in the poem.
3. What effect is created by the constant repetition of the word
   hammers? How does this effect contribute to the poem's meaning? What is the effect of the repeated "night and day" in lines
   3 and 8?
4. Compare this poem with Sandburg's "Prayers of Steel." How do
   the two poems differ in mood? Which poem is more hopeful?
   More vigorous? More realistic?

Fable

STEPHEN CRANE

In heaven
Some little blades of grass
Stood before God.
"What did you do?"
Then all save one of the little blades   5
Began eagerly to relate
The merits of their lives.
This one stayed a small way behind,
Ashamed.

Presently, God said,   10
"And what did *you* do?"
The little blade answered, "O my Lord,
Memory is bitter to me,
For if I did good deeds
I know not of them."   15
Then God, in all his splendor,
Arose from his throne.
"O best little blade of grass!" he said.

1. Which blade of grass did God consider the best? Why? What
   idea was the poet expressing?
2. Look up the meaning of *fable*. Tell why this is, or is not, a good
   example of a fable.
3. Note the simplicity with which this poet has expressed his idea.
   What effect does this simplicity of style have upon you? Would
   you have preferred a more elaborate style? Explain.

Without a Cloak

PHYLLIS McGINLEY

Hate has a fashionable cut.
 It is the garment man agrees on,
Snug, colorful, the proper weight
 For comfort in an icy season.

And it is weatherproof, they say—   5
 Becoming, also, to the spirit.
I fetched Hate homeward yesterday,
 But there it hangs. I cannot wear it.

It is a dress that suits me ill,
 However much the mode sustains me.   10
At once too ample and too small,
 It trips, bewilders, and confines me.

And in my blood do fevers flow,
 Corruptive, where the fabric presses,
Till I must pluck it off as though   15
 It were the burning shirt of Nessus.

Proud walk the people folded warm
 In Hate. They need not pray for spring.
But threadbare do I face the storm
 Or hug my hearthstone, shivering.   20

1. The poet compares Hate to a garment. How is the metaphor built up through the poem?
2. Read the final stanza. Does the poet mean that those who can hate are better off than those who cannot? Explain.
3. When Hercules put on the magic shirt of Nessus the centaur, it poisoned his flesh. Suffering horrible agony because he was unable to remove the shirt, Hercules killed himself.

Fire and Ice

ROBERT FROST

Some say the world will end in fire,
Some say in ice.
From what I've tasted of desire
I hold with those who favor fire.
But if it had to perish twice,   5
I think I know enough of hate
To say that for destruction ice
Is also great
And would suffice.

1. What do the words *fire* and *ice* suggest to you? The poet associates "taste" and "desire" with fire, and "know" and "hate" with ice. What aspect of man's nature is connected with "desiring"; what aspect with "knowing"? What does the poet imply will cause the destruction of the world? What do fire and ice symbolize?
2. Examine the structure of the poem. Why would longer lines be more appropriate to the discussion of fire? Why would shorter lines and rather flat statements be more appropriate for ice?

Caliban in the Coal Mines

LOUIS UNTERMEYER

God, we don't like to complain,
   We know that the mine is no lark.
But—there's the pools from the rain;
   But—there's the cold and the dark.

God, You don't know what it is—   5
   You, in Your well-lighted sky—
Watching the meteors whizz;
   Warm, with the sun always by.

God, if You had but the moon
   Stuck in Your cap for a lamp,   10
Even You'd tire of it soon,
   Down in the dark and the damp.

Nothing but blackness above
   And nothing that moves but the cars . . .
God, if You wish for our love,   15
   Fling us a handful of stars!

1. Would you describe this poem as a prayer? If so, what does the
   miner pray for?
2. Who was Caliban? Why is it an appropriate name for the coal
   miner?
3. A "handful of stars" is a symbol. What do you think it stands for?

fate is unfair

DON MARQUIS

in many places here and
there
i think that fate
is quite unfair
yon centipede upon
the floor
can boast of
tootsies by the score
consider my
distressing fix
my feet are limited
to six
did i a hundred
feet possess
would all that glorious
footfulness
enable me
to stagger less
when i am
overcome by heat

or if i had
a hundred feet
would i
careering oer the floor
stagger
proportionately more
well i suppose
the mind serene
will not tell
destiny its mean
the truly
philosophic mind
will use
such feet as it can find
and follow calmly
fast or slow
the feet it has
where eer they go
                    archy

1. This poem, like "Fire and Ice," states a profound idea with utmost simplicity. What is the idea expressed in this poem?
2. How does "the truly philosophic mind" deal with the seeming unfairness of fate? Describe your reaction to bad luck.
3. Archy, a character by Marquis, is a cockroach that writes on the typewriter at night. How does this explain the lack of capital letters in the poem?

To the Stone-Cutters

ROBINSON JEFFERS

Stone-cutters fighting time with marble, you foredefeated
Challengers of oblivion
Eat cynical earnings, knowing rock splits, records fall down
The square-limbed Roman letters
Scale in the thaw, wear in the rain. The poet as well   5
Builds his monument mockingly;
For man will be blotted out, the blithe earth die, the brave sun
Die blind and blacken to the heart.
Yet stones have stood for a thousand years, and pained thoughts
   found
The honey of peace in old poems.   10

1. Before you begin to discuss this poem, be sure you know the
   meanings of *foredefeated*, *oblivion*, and *cynical*. Why, according
   to the poem, are the stone-cutters "foredefeated"? What makes
   their earnings "cynical"? What is the full significance of the word
   fighting as it is used in the context of this poem?
2. In what respect is a poet like a stone-cutter? What is a poet's
   monument? Explain the statement "The poet as well/Builds his
   monument mockingly."
3. What shift in thought occurs after the word *yet*? Does Jeffers
   really. think the poet and the stone-cutters are "foredefeated"?
   Explain.

Parting Gift

ELINOR WYLIE

I cannot give you the Metropolitan Tower;
I cannot give you heaven;
Nor the nine Visigoth crowns in the Cluny Museum;
Nor happiness, even.
But I can give you a very small purse   5
Made out of field-mouse skin,
With a painted picture of the universe
And seven blue tears therein.

I cannot give you the island of Capri;
I cannot give you beauty;   10
Nor bake you marvelous crusty cherry pies
With love and duty.
But I can give you a very little locket
Made out of wildcat hide:
Put it into your left-hand pocket   15
And never look inside.

1. Tell why you feel that the parting gifts of the speaker are, or are
   not, valuable. What makes certain gifts important to you while
   others are valueless?
2. This poem achieves a touching quality by combining sophistica-
   tion with childishness. How is this brought out in the nature of
   the gifts and in what the speaker instructs the receiver to do with
   the last one?
3. How would you describe the character of the speaker in this poem?
   Point to those lines which helped to form your opinion.

Transcontinent

DONALD HALL

Where the cities end, the
dumps grow the oil-can shacks
from Portland, Maine,

to Seattle. Broken
cars rust in Troy, New York,   5
and Cleveland Heights.

On the train, the people
eat candy bars, and watch,
or fall asleep.

When they look outside and   10
see cars and shacks, they know
they're nearly there.

1. This poem was written in 1959. What subject of contemporary
   interest does it deal with?
2. What impression of the country does this poem give? What
   words are particularly effective in building up the images?
3. How does the poet get across to his readers that he is describing
   much of the country, not just a small area? What is the reaction
   of the people to what is all around them? What would you say
   was the poet's attitude toward the condition of the land and the
   people he mentions?

Kitchenette Building

GWENDOLYN BROOKS

We are things of dry hours and the involuntary plan,
Grayed in, and gray. "Dream" makes a giddy sound, not strong
Like "rent," "feeding a wife," "satisfying a man."

But could a dream send up through onion fumes
Its white and violet, fight with fried potatoes   5
And yesterday's garbage ripening in the hall,
Flutter, or sing an aria down these rooms.

Even if we were willing to let it in,
Had time to warm it, keep it very clean,
Anticipate a message, let it begin?   10

We wonder. But not well! not for a minute!
Since Number Five is out of the bathroom now,
We think of lukewarm water, hope to get in it.

1. What kind of people are the "we" in this poem? Which specific
   physical details in the poem help to identify their circumstances?
2. The nature of the lives led by the persons in the poem is further
   suggested through poetic images. What is the significance of "dry
   hour"; of "involuntary plan"; of "grayed in, and gray"?
3. What is the implication of lines 2–3, beginning with "Dream
   makes a giddy sound"?
4. Discuss separately the effect of stanzas 2, 3, and 4 in intensifying
   our feeling about the lives of the people in the poem.
5. How is your reaction to the poem affected by knowledge that
   Gwendolyn Brooks is a black poet who lived most of her life in
   the city of Chicago?

Auto Wreck

KARL SHAPIRO

Its quick soft silver bell beating, beating,
And down the dark one ruby flare
Pulsing out red light like an artery,
The ambulance at top speed floating down
Past beacons and illuminated clocks   5
Wings in a heavy curve, dips down,
And brakes speed, entering the crowd.
The doors leap open, emptying light;
Stretchers are laid out, the mangled lifted
And stowed into the little hospital.   10
Then the bell, breaking the hush, tolls once,
And the ambulance with its terrible cargo
Rocking, slightly rocking, moves away,
As the doors, an afterthought, are closed.

We are deranged, walking among the cops   15
Who sweep glass and are large and composed.
One is still making notes under the light.
One with a bucket douches ponds of blood
Into the street and gutter.
One hangs lanterns on the wrecks that cling,   20
Empty husks of locusts, to iron poles.

Our throats were tight as tourniquets,
Our feet were bound with splints, but now,
Like convalescents intimate and gauche,°   awkward
We speak through sickly smiles and warn   25
With the stubborn saw ° of common sense,   saying
The grim joke and the banal ° resolution.   commonplace
The traffic moves around with care,
But we remain, touching a wound
That opens to our richest horror.   30

Already old, the question Who shall die?
Becomes unspoken Who is innocent?
For death in war is done by hands;
Suicide has cause and still birth, logic;
And cancer, simple as a flower, blooms.   35
But this invites the occult ° mind,   hidden, secret
Cancels our physics with a sneer,
And spatters all we knew of denouement °   conclusion, ending
Across the expedient and wicked stones.

1. The idea behind this poem is stated in the final stanza. What
   question is the poet trying to answer? Explain in your own words
   lines 36-39.
2. Did the speaker in this poem play a part in the auto wreck or was
   he just an observer? Point to lines which support your answer.
3. Why is there a break in the poem after line 14? What is the
   purpose of the first fourteen lines?
4. Select the most vivid of the poem's images. What effect do they
   have on you? Point out examples of figurative language. What
   is consistent about the imagery in this poem?

A Pilot from the Carrier

RANDALL JARRELL

Strapped at the center of the blazing wheel,
His flesh ice-white against the shattered mask,
He tears at the easy clasp, his sobbing breaths
Misting the fresh blood lightening to flame,
Darkening to smoke; trapped there in pain   5
And fire and breathlessness, he struggles free
Into the sunlight of the upper sky—
And falls, a quiet bundle in the sky,
The miles to warmth, to air, to waking:
To the great flowering of his life, the hemisphere   10
That holds his dangling years. In its long, slow sway
The world steadies and is almost still . . .
He is alone; and hangs in knowledge
Slight, separate, estranged: a lonely eye
Reading a child's first scrawl, the carrier's wake—   15
The travelling milk-like circle of a miss
Beside the plant-like genius of the smoke
That shades, on the little deck, the little blaze
Toy-like as the glitter of the wing-guns,
Shining as the fragile sun-marked plane   20
That grows to him, rubbed silver tipped with flame.

1. This poem describes what happens to a pilot whose plane has
   been hit in an air battle. Tell briefly what has apparently happened, what is happening as the poem proceeds, and what is
   likely to happen finally to the pilot.

2. What images make you aware of the pilot's total aloneness in his plight?
3. What are the implications of the phrase "a quiet bundle in the sky" (line 8)?
4. What does the speaker mean when he says that this "quiet bundle" falls "to waking," to "the great flowering of his life"?
5. How do the carrier and the plane appear to the falling pilot? What is the effect of such phrases and words as "a child's first scrawl," "little deck," "Toy-like," "fragile"? How are all these images related to the description in lines 8–12?
6. Who is the *speaker* in this poem? How would you describe *his* tone? Does it seem appropriate or inappropriate to the actual content of the poem?

Of Modern Poetry

WALLACE STEVENS

The poem of the mind in the act of finding
What will suffice. It has not always had
To find: the scene was set; it repeated what
Was in the script.
              Then the theatre was changed   5
To something else. Its past was a souvenir.

It has to be living, to learn the speech of the place.
It has to face the men of the time and to meet
The women of the time. It has to think about war
And it has to find what will suffice. It has   10
To construct a new stage. It has to be on that stage
And, like an insatiable° actor, slowly and   not to be satisfied
With meditation speak words that in the ear,

In the delicatest ear of the mind, repeat,
Exactly, that which it wants to hear, at the sound   15
Of which, an invisible audience listens,
Not to the play, but to itself, expressed
In an emotion as of two people, as of two
Emotions becoming one. The actor is
A metaphysician in the dark, twanging   20
An instrument, twanging a wiry string that gives
Sounds passing through sudden rightnesses, wholly
Containing the mind, below which it cannot descend,
Beyond which it has no will to rise.
                                      It must   25
Be the finding of a satisfaction, and may
Be of a man skating, a woman dancing, a woman
Combing. The poem of the act of the mind.

1. According to the speaker in this poem, what differences should
   there be between modern poetry and the poetry of the past?
2. Describe the metaphor that the poet builds through the poem.
   With what does he identify modern poetry?
3. In lines 13–19 the poet describes the relationship that ought to
   exist between the reader and the poem. How would you describe
   that relationship? What does the speaker mean when he says the
   "audience listens . . . to itself . . . as of two people, as of two/
   Emotions becoming one"?
4. In lines 25–28, the speaker briefly alludes to the subjects appropriate to modern poetry. What do these subjects have in common? Why are they appropriate today? How might they be "the
   finding of a satisfaction"? How might they have the effect
   described earlier in lines 20-24?

The Groundhog

RICHARD EBERHART

In June, amid the golden fields,
I saw a groundhog lying dead.
Dead lay he; my senses shook,
And mind outshot our naked frailty.
There lowly in the vigorous summer   5
His form began its senseless change,
And made my senses waver dim
Seeing nature ferocious in him.
Inspecting close his maggots' might
And seething cauldron of his being,   10
Half with loathing, half with a strange love,
I poked him with an angry stick.
The fever arose, became a flame
And Vigour circumscribed the skies,
Immense energy in the sun,   15
And through my frame a sunless trembling.
My stick had done nor good nor harm.
Then stood I silent in the day
Watching the object, as before;
And kept my reverence for knowledge   20
Trying for control, to be still,
To quell the passion of the blood;
Until I had bent down on my knees
Praying for joy in the sight of decay.
And so I left; and I returned   25
In Autumn strict of eye, to see
The sap gone out of the groundhog,

But the bony sodden hulk remained.
But the year had lost its meaning,
And in intellectual chains   30
I lost both love and loathing,
Mured ° up in the wall of wisdom.   closed
Another summer took the fields again
Massive and burning, full of life,
But when I chanced upon the spot   35
There was only a little hair left,
And bones bleaching in the sunlight
Beautiful as architecture;
I watched them like a geometer,
And cut a walking stick from a birch.   40
It has been three years, now.
There is no sign of the groundhog.
I stood there in the whirling summer,
My hand capped a withered heart,
And thought of China and of Greece,   45
Of Alexander in his tent;
Of Montaigne in his tower,
Of Saint Theresa in her wild lament.

1. What is the occasion of this poem? How many times did the
   speaker visit the same spot? Describe his reactions on each occasion. How might the times of his visits have affected his mood?
2. What has happened to the speaker to bring about the intense feeling expressed in line 44? What human concern has been aroused
   in him by his observance of the dead groundhog and its disintegra-
   tion? Why, when he thinks of China, Greece, Alexander, Montaigne, and St. Theresa, does his hand cap a "withered heart"?
   What has happened to these people and places? What fate do
   they share with the groundhog?

POEMS
FOR STUDY
AND ENJOYMENT

Go, Lovely Rose!

EDMUND WALLER

Go, lovely Rose!
Tell her that wastes her time and me,
　　That now she knows,
When I resemble her to thee,
How sweet and fair she seems to be.　　　　　　5

　　Tell her that's young,
And shuns to have her graces spied,
　　That hadst thou sprung
In deserts, where no men abide,
Thou must have uncommended died.　　　　　　10

　　Small is the worth
Of beauty from the light retired;
　　Bid her come forth,
Suffer herself to be desired,
And not blush so to be admired.　　　　　　15

　　Then die! that she
The common fate of all things rare
　　May read in thee;
How small a part of time they share
That are so wondrous sweet and fair!　　　　　　20

Sonnet 29

WILLIAM SHAKESPEARE

When, in disgrace with fortune and men's eyes,
I all alone beweep my outcast state,
And trouble deaf heaven with my bootless° cries,   useless
And look upon myself, and curse my fate,
Wishing me like to one more rich in hope,   5
Featured like him, like him with friends possessed,
Desiring this man's art and that man's scope,
With what I most enjoy contented least;
Yet in these thoughts myself almost despising,
Haply° I think on thee—and then my state,   fortunately 10
Like to the lark at break of day arising
From sullen earth, sings hymns at heaven's gate;
    For thy sweet love remembered such wealth brings
    That then I scorn to change my state with kings.

Frederick Douglass

ROBERT E. HAYDEN

When it is finally ours, this freedom, this liberty, this beautiful
and terrible thing, needful to man as air,
usable as earth; when it belongs at last to all,
when it is truly instinct, brain matter, diastole, systole,
reflex action; when it is finally won; when it is more   5
than the gaudy mumbo jumbo of politicians:
this man, this Douglass, this former slave, this Negro
beaten to his knees, exiled, visioning a world
where none is lonely, none hunted, alien,
this man, superb in love and logic, this man   10
shall be remembered. Oh, not with statues' rhetoric,
not with legends and poems and wreaths of bronze alone,
but with the lives grown out of his life, the lives
fleshing his dream of the beautiful, needful thing.

Frederick Douglass, born a slave, escaped from slavery after many
cruel experiences. He became a renowned abolitionist speaker in New
England, was consulted by President Lincoln during the Civil War,
and ultimately held high posts in the United States government. He
was always in the forefront of the struggle for equal rights for black
people.

Petit, the Poet

EDGAR LEE MASTERS

Seeds in a dry pod, tick, tick, tick,
Tick, tick, tick, like mites in a quarrel—
Faint iambics that the full breeze wakens—
But the pine tree makes a symphony thereof.
Triolets, villanelles, rondels, rondeaus,   5
Ballades by the score with the same old thought:
The snows and the roses of yesterday are vanished;
And what is love but a rose that fades?
Life all around me here in the village:
Tragedy, comedy, valor and truth,   10
Courage, constancy, heroism, failure—
All in the loom, and oh what patterns!
Woodlands, meadows, streams and rivers—
Blind to all of it all my life long.
Triolets, villanelles, rondels, rondeaus,   15
Seeds in a dry pod, tick, tick, tick,
Tick, tick, tick, what little iambics,
While Homer and Whitman roared in the pines!

Ulysses

ALFRED, LORD TENNYSON

It little profits that an idle king,
By this still hearth, among these barren crags,
Matched with an aged wife, I mete and dole
Unequal laws unto a savage race,
That hoard, and sleep, and feed, and know not me.   5
I cannot rest from travel; I will drink
Life to the lees. All times I have enjoyed
Greatly, have suffered greatly, both with those
That loved me, and alone; on shore, and when
Through scudding drifts the rainy Hyades   10
Vexed the dim sea. I am become a name;
For always roaming with a hungry heart
Much have I seen and known—cities of men
And manners, climates, councils, governments,
Myself not least, but honored of them all—   15
And drunk delight of battle with my peers,
Far on the ringing plains of windy Troy.
I am a part of all that I have met;
Yet all experience is an arch wherethrough
Gleams that untraveled world whose margin fades   20
Forever and forever when I move.
How dull it is to pause, to make an end,
To rust unburnished, not to shine in use!
As though to breathe were life! Life piled on life
Were all too little, and of one to me   25
Little remains; but every hour is saved
From eternal silence, something more,

A bringer of new things; and vile it were
For some three suns to store and hoard myself,
And this gray spirit yearning in desire   30
To follow knowledge like a sinking star,
Beyond the utmost bound of human thought.
    This is my son, mine own Telemachus,
To whom I leave the scepter and the isle—
Well-loved of me, discerning to fulfill   35
This labor, by slow prudence to make mild
A rugged people, and through soft degrees
Subdue them to the useful and the good.
Most blameless is he, centered in the sphere
Of common duties, decent not to fail   40
In offices of tenderness, and pay
Meet adoration to my household gods,
When I am gone. He works his work, I mine.
    There lies the port; the vessel puffs her sail;
There gloom the dark, broad seas. My mariners,   45
Souls that have toiled, and wrought, and thought with me—
That ever with a frolic welcome took
The thunder and the sunshine, and opposed
Free hearts, free foreheads—you and I are old;
Old age hath yet his honor and his toil.   50
Death closes all; but something ere the end,
Some work of noble note, may yet be done,
Not unbecoming men that strove with gods.
The lights begin to twinkle from the rocks;
The long day wanes; the slow moon climbs; the deep   55
Moans round with many voices. Come, my friends,
'Tis not too late to seek a newer world.
Push off, and sitting well in order smite
The sounding furrows; for my purpose holds
To sail beyond the sunset, and the baths   60
Of all the western stars, until I die.

It may be that the gulfs will wash us down;
It may be we shall touch the Happy Isles,
And see the great Achilles, whom we knew.
Though much is taken, much abides; and though 65
We are not now that strength which in old days
Moved earth and heaven, that which we are, we are—
One equal temper of heroic hearts,
Made weak by time and fate, but strong in will
To strive, to seek, to find, and not to yield. 70

Outer Drive

EDWIN HONIG

Heat of nightfall, and the heave and start,
Beside a quivering sleek trolley on the track,
Of a sudden snub-cabbed truck, trailerless,
Intense; like a bullhead bodiless it rockets
Just grazing past the green tan flank 5
Of the wincing public car, lit up with heads
Featured in the window squares, going
Straight and ironbound, by safety islands,
Down the flickering neon evening, home—

While the deathless disembodied bullhead of a truck 10
Escapes: past stoplights raging, headlights steaming
Rips through city limits eating, eating,
Eating all the highway up to Albany.

The Listeners

WALTER DE LA MARE

"Is there anybody there?" said the Traveler,
    Knocking on the moonlit door;
And his horse in the silence champed the grasses
    Of the forest's ferny floor;
And a bird flew up out of the turret,   5
    Above the Traveler's head;
And he smote upon the door again a second time;
    "Is there anybody there?" he said.
But no one descended to the Traveler;
    No head from the leaf-fringed sill   10
Leaned over and looked into his gray eyes,
    Where he stood perplexed and still.
But only a host of phantom listeners
    That dwelt in the lone house then
Stood listening in the quiet of the moonlight   15
    To that voice from the world of men:
Stood thronging the faint moonbeams on the dark stair,
    That goes down to the empty hall,
Hearkening in an air stirred and shaken
    By the lonely Traveler's call.   20
And he felt in his heart their strangeness,
    Their stillness answering his cry,

While his horse moved, cropping the dark turf,
    'Neath the starred and leafy sky;
For he suddenly smote on the door, even   25
    Louder, and lifted his head:
"Tell them I came, and no one answered,
    That I kept my word," he said.
Never the least stir made the listeners,
    Though every word he spake   30
Fell echoing through the shadowiness of the still house
    From the one man left awake:
Ay, they heard his foot upon the stirrup,
    And the sound of iron on stone,
And how the silence surged softly backward,   35
    When the plunging hoofs were gone.

Limited

CARL SANDBURG

I am riding on a limited express, one of the crack trains of the
    nation.
Hurtling across the prairie into blue haze and dark air go fifteen
    all-steel coaches holding a thousand people.
(All the coaches shall be scrap and rust and all the men and
    women laughing in the diners and sleepers shall pass to ashes.)
I ask a man in the smoker where he is going and he answers:
    "Omaha."

The Negro Speaks of Rivers

LANGSTON HUGHES

I've known rivers:
I've known rivers ancient as the world and older than the
    flow of human blood in human veins.

My soul has grown deep like the rivers.

I bathed in the Euphrates when dawns were young.
I built my hut near the Congo and it lulled me to sleep.   **5**
I looked upon the Nile and raised the pyramids above it.
I heard the singing of the Mississippi when Abe Lincoln went
    down to New Orleans, and I've seen its muddy bosom turn all
    golden in the sunset.

Constantly risking absurdity

LAWRENCE FERLINGHETTI

Constantly risking absurdity
               and death
      whenever he performs
            above the heads
                of his audience   **5**
the poet like an acrobat
         climbs on rime
           to a high wire of his own making
and balancing on eyebeams
          above a sea of faces   **10**
      paces his way
         to the other side of day
performing entrechats°   **in ballet,**
        and sleight-of-foot tricks   **an intricate leap**
and other high theatrics   **15**
         and all without mistaking
    any thing
       for what it may not be

For he's the super realist
                        who must perforce perceive   20
                taut truth
                        before the taking of each stance or step
in his supposed advance
                        toward that still higher perch
where Beauty stands and waits   25
                        with gravity
                                to start her death-defying leap
        And he
                a little charleychaplin man
                                who may or may not catch   30
                        her fair eternal form
                                spreadeagled in the empty air
                of existence

About the Poets

Elizabeth Bishop (1911–   ) has won many honors and awards for her poetry, including the Pulitzer Prize in 1956. Born in Worcester, Massachusetts, Miss Bishop makes her home in Rio de Janeiro. She is currently working on a book which deals with cultural life in Brazil. Her most recent volume of poetry was called *Questions of Travel*.

Rupert Brooke (1887–1915) was educated at Cambridge and traveled extensively after his graduation from college. At the outbreak of World War I, he enlisted in the British Expeditionary Force. Many of his poems are based upon his war experiences and reflect his romantic idealism. He died of blood poisoning en route to the Dardanelles and was buried on the isle of Skyros in the Aegean Sea. The prophecy of his famous sonnet, "The Soldier," was fulfilled, for he was buried in "some corner of a foreign field that is forever England."

Gwendolyn Brooks (1917–   ) was born in Topeka, Kansas, but has lived most of her life in Chicago, where she teaches now at the Chicago Teachers College. She received the Pulitzer Prize for poetry in 1950. Her most recent book, published in 1972, is a series of biographical vignettes called *Report From Part One*, explaining her commitment, since the assassination of Martin Luther King, Jr., to a more active stance in the cause of civil rights for black people. She has conducted poetry classes among some of the black teen-age gangs in the Chicago area.

Elizabeth Barrett Browning (1806–1861) was born in Durham, England, the daughter of a rich landowner. She began writing poetry at an early age and became a fluent scholar of Greek and Latin. Though her delicate health forced her to live in retirement for many years, she contributed poems to periodicals, thus establishing her reputation as a poet. She met Robert Browning in 1845, and despite her father's opposition, married him the following year. Miss Browning spent the greater part of her married life in Italy. Her most famous book of poems is *Sonnets from the Portuguese*.

Robert Browning (1812–1889) was one of the leading Victorian poets. Educated by private tutors, Browning came under the spell of Shelley and Keats at an early age. He married Elizabeth Barrett in 1846, and their happy years together constitute one of the great romances of English literature. Browning's poetry has sometimes been described as difficult and obscure. He is said to have remarked about a difficult section in one of his poems, "When that passage was written only God and Robert Browning knew what it meant. Now only God knows." Browning is a poet who speaks with vigor and optimism, reflecting a hopeful and enthusiastic approach to life.

William Cullen Bryant (1794–1878) spent many years practicing law before he became a full-time writer and one of the first American poets to win recognition here and abroad. Born in Cummington, Massachusetts, the son of a country doctor, Bryant began writing poetry at an early age. He published his first poem in a small-town newspaper at the age of ten. The publication of his poem "Thanatopsis," and the popular acclaim it achieved, led to his appointment as editor-in-chief of the *New York Evening Post*, a position he held for more than fifty years. One of his best-known poems is "To a Waterfowl."

Robert Burns (1759–1796) is best known for his beautiful love lyrics and for poems which reveal his affection for the small, everyday things in nature. He was the son of a humble farmer who encouraged in his children a respect and an enthusiasm for learning. Burns devoted himself to the writing of poetry which eventually brought him fame but little money. During his last days he was beset by ill health and debts. He died at the early age of thirty-seven in Dumfries, Scotland.

Bliss Carman (1861–1929) was born in Canada but spent most of his life in the United States. He received the major part of his formal education here, and it was at Harvard that he met Richard Hovey with whom he wrote the *Vagabondia* poems, published in three volumes. In the years that followed he wrote more than twenty volumes of light and carefree verse.

Lewis Carroll (1832–1898) was the pen name of Charles Lutwidge Dodgson, an obscure lecturer in mathematics at Oxford, who is now world famous as the author of *Alice in Wonderland* and *Through the Looking-Glass*. Both were written especially for children, but they have charmed readers of all ages and in many countries with their humor and tongue-in-cheek observations about life.

Hilda Conkling (1910–   ) is the daughter of Grace Hazard Conkling, a distinguished teacher and poet. Miss Conkling showed great talent even as a child, and before she was twelve had written two volumes of poetry. "When Moonlight Falls" is one of her early poems.

Stephen Crane (1871–1900), the fourteenth son of a minister, was orphaned at eighteen, and lived as a penniless writer in a New York slum until he was twenty-three. The success of his Civil War novel, *The Red Badge of Courage*, secured him work as a journalist and war correspondent. In his life, which was tragically shortened by tuberculosis, he wrote several works considered by some to be shaping forces in modern American writing. Crane's poems appeared in two volumes, *The Black Riders* and *War Is Kind*.

Adelaide Crapsey (1878–1914) wrote most of her poems in a sanitarium during the last few months of her life. Following her graduation from Vassar College, she traveled abroad, studied archeology in Rome, and taught literature and poetry in the United States. She has been called the inventor of the "cinquain," a five line, unrhymed stanza. A year after her death her poems were published in a thin volume entitled *Verse*.

Countee Cullen (1903–1946) was born in New York City, the son of a Methodist minister. He started writing poetry early and achieved some notice in a number of magazines. He received his A.B. degree from New York University in 1925, his M.A. from Harvard in 1926. For a time he was assistant editor of a Negro journal, then held a Guggenheim fellowship for travel and study abroad. He spent the last eleven years of his life teaching French in high school. Among his works are *Color*, *The Lost Zoo*, *My Lives and How I Lost Them*.

Edward Estlin Cummings (1894–1962) based his first book, *The Enormous Room*, on an experience he had during World War I when he was imprisoned on suspicion of being a spy. After the war he studied painting in Paris, and then returned to New York to find himself popularly recognized for his first volume of poems, *Tulips and Chimneys*. He received the Dial Award for distinguished service to American letters in

1925. In 1952, Cummings returned to Harvard, his alma mater, as the Charles Eliot Norton Professor of Poetry. He was elected a member of the American Academy of Arts and Letters and, in 1957, received the Bollingen Prize in Poetry. Unlike many poets, Cummings was able to earn his living through the reading of his poems or the sale of them.

Mary Carolyn Davies, an American writer and author of verse, has contributed poems to many magazines, including the *Saturday Evening Post.* (The editor regrets that additional biographical information was not available.)

Walter de la Mare (1873–1956) began his literary career by starting a school magazine at St. Paul's Cathedral School in London where he received his education. At the time his first short story appeared he was working as a clerk in the London office of an oil company. Several years later, a grant from the British government and a small pension enabled him to devote full time to writing. Much of de la Mare's poetry and prose can be appreciated by children as well as adults. His style is simple and delicate, often conveying a mood both whimsical and fantastic.

Emily Dickinson (1830–1886) ranks as one of the world's most talented poets. With the exception of one short trip to Washington and Philadelphia, and another to Boston, she spent all her life in Amherst, Massachusetts. She rarely went beyond her garden gate and saw only her family and a few intimate friends. Miss Dickinson wrote many poems about life, death, love and nature. Almost all of her poetry remained unpublished until after her death.

John Donne (1573–1631) was one of the leaders of the metaphysical school of poetry which flourished in England during the seventeenth century. He was educated at both Oxford and Cambridge, became an ordained Anglican minister, and was considered the greatest preacher of his time. Among his many poems is the sonnet "Death, Be Not Proud."

Richard Eberhart (1904–   ) was born in Austin, Minnesota and studied at Dartmouth, Cambridge University (England) and Harvard. At one time he held an executive post in a large business firm. The major part of his life has been devoted to writing poetry and lecturing at several large universities. He received the Pulitzer Prize in 1966, and is currently teaching at Dartmouth.

Lawrence Ferlinghetti (1919–   ) was born in Yonkers, New York and studied at Columbia University. Although he was a commanding officer in the U. S. Navy during World War II, he has more recently been active in anti–war demonstrations. He has been a major figure among new poets who have expressed strong antagonism toward established institutions in our country, and has been personally instrumental in getting the work of young poets published and sold. Mr. Ferlinghetti is a prolific writer, publishing new works almost every year.

Robert Frost (1875–1963) was awarded the Pulitzer Prize several times and justly won the title of "Dean of American Poets." In addition to writing poetry, he taught school, farmed, and edited a country newspaper. His poetry, which is simple and realistic, embodies the spirit of New England. In 1961, Frost had the distinction of being the first poet ever to participate in a presidential inauguration.

Hamlin Garland (1860–1940) left teaching and prospecting in the Middle West and traveled to Boston to embark on a literary career. But the "middle border" farm country where he grew up is the setting for many of his books, including his novel, *A Son of the Middle Border,* which has been called one of the finest examples of regional literature.

William S. Gilbert (1836–1911) wrote librettos for the many famous Gilbert and Sullivan operettas, including *The Mikado, The Pirates of Penzance,* and *H.M.S. Pinafore.* At the age of thirteen, Gilbert left school to work in the theater but eventually completed his education, graduating as valedictorian of his class. His famous association with Arthur Sullivan lasted for over twenty years. As a librettist, Gilbert was noted for his clever rhyming, fantastic plots, and good-humored satire.

Oliver Goldsmith (1728–1774) tried unsuccessfully to establish a medical practice in London until, desperate for money, he turned to doing literary hack work. He finally gained recognition as a writer and became a member of the famous literary club presided over by Samuel Johnson. Goldsmith died at the age of forty-six, having written one outstanding work in each of the major fields of literature. These include the novel, *The Vicar of Wakefield,* the play, *She Stoops to Conquer,* and the poem, "The Deserted Village "

Arthur Guiterman (1871–1943) is perhaps best known for his humorous verses and American ballads. Born in Austria of American parents, he came to the United States where he received his education and then embarked on a career in journalism. He also wrote librettos for several operas, notably Walter Damrosch's opera, *The Man without a Country.*

Donald Hall (1928–　　) was born in New Haven, Connecticut. Educated at Harvard and Oxford, he now teaches in the English Department of the University of Michigan. A well-recognized poet himself, and recipient of various awards for his work, he has also edited several important anthologies of poetry, including one of contemporary American poetry.

Robert Hayden (1913–　　) was born in Detroit, Michigan. He has taught at the University of Michigan and at Fisk University, and he has won many awards for his poetry, notably a Ford Foundation grant in 1954. Many of his poems deal with the history of black people in America up to the present time. He has edited a well–known anthology of poems by black writers called *Kaleidoscope.* A collection of poems called *Words in Mourning Time* is his most recent publication.

Ralph Hodgson (1872–1962) was born in Yorkshire, England. Early in his career he was a magazine editor and publisher of pamphlets. Later he lectured on English literature in a Japanese university. He received several awards for his poetry. From 1942 until his death he lived in the United States in Ohio, breeding dogs and writing occasional poetry.

Oliver Wendell Holmes (1809–1894) was by profession a professor of anatomy and physiology and later was appointed Dean of the Harvard Medical School. Through his contributions to the *Atlantic Monthly,* he won recognition as a poet and essayist. His most famous poem, "Old Ironsides," was written as a protest when it was announced that the *Constitution,* a frigate of the War of 1812, was to be destroyed in the Charleston Navy Yard. This poem saved the ship and made Holmes famous.

Edwin Honig (1919–　　) teaches now at Brown University. He is known both as an original poet and a literary scholar and critic. He was educated at the University of Wisconsin.

Alfred Edward Housman (1859–1936) was the author of one of the most widely read volumes of poetry, *A Shropshire Lad*, published in 1896. Educated at Oxford, he taught at the University of London and at Cambridge and soon gained a reputation as a critic and poet of keen intellect. Housman's poems have the classic dignity of Greek poetry and the simplicity and honesty characteristic of the best in English poetry. Friendship, mortality, and the vanity of human wishes are his predominant themes.

Langston Hughes (1902–1967), one of America's most significant black poets, was born in Joplin, Missouri, moved to Illinois, then to Ohio, and finally reached Columbia University. He left Columbia without a degree, took up a sailor's life which carried him throughout the world, worked at odd jobs in New York City, finally completing his education at Lincoln University in Pennsylvania, in 1929. His first poetry success came in 1925, and he followed it with works of fiction, biography, history, humor, and other poetry. Among his published works are *The Weary Blues*, *Shakespeare in Harlem*, and *Selected Poems*.

Leigh Hunt (1784–1859) embarked, at an early age, on a journalistic career but later turned to poetry as his chief means of expression. A friend of both Keats and Shelley, Hunt became one of the controversial figures of his day. His radical outlook made him a friend of all liberal movements, and he once spent two years in prison for calling the Prince-Regent unflattering names, "Abou Ben Adhem" is perhaps his most famous poem.

Randall Jarrell (1914–1965) was born in Nashville, Tennessee, and educated at Vanderbilt University. He served for three and a half years in the Army Air Force during World War II, where he was to experience the horror of war that he would later record in many of his poems. He taught at many universities, was Consultant in Poetry at the Library of Congress, and served as literary editor of *The Nation*, but it was as a poet that he was best known. At the time of his death in an automobile accident, he was living with his wife and two daughters in Greensboro, North Carolina, and teaching English at the University of North Carolina.

Robinson Jeffers (1887–1962), born in Pittsburgh, lived most of his adult life in Carmel, California, on the Monterey Peninsula. This land of wild natural changes has been a focal point in many of his works. Jeffers was influenced greatly by the psychoanalytic theories of Freud and Jung, and the greater part of his work deals with the inner compulsions and passions which motivate man's baser actions. His work is often violent, harsh, and tormented.

James Weldon Johnson (1871–1938), born in Jacksonville, Florida, received a B.A. and M.A. at Atlanta University. His career was a rich one, including the practice of law, the writing of successful popular songs in collaboration with his brother, acting as U. S. Consul to Venezuela and later to Nicaragua, and the teaching of literature at Fisk University and at New York University. One of his most popular works was a novel, *The Autobiography of an Ex-Colored Man*, which he published anonymously.

John Keats (1795–1821), the son of a livery stable keeper, ranks among the greatest poets of English literature, as well as of world literature. His family wanted him to become a surgeon, but at the age of twenty-two Keats decided to devote his life to writing. A friendship at school with the headmaster's son was greatly responsible for his decision. Keats died of consumption at the pathetically youthful age of twenty-six, having written all of his great poetry in the remarkably short span of five years. On his grave is inscribed the verse, "Here lies one whose name was writ in water."

Alfred Kreymborg (1896–1966) was born in New York City. His interest in the underdog and social progress was always evident in his poetry and in his biography called *Troubadour*. He edited several poetry anthologies and was once president of the Poetry Society of America, but he never graduated from high school.

Vachel Lindsay (1879–1931) attended Hiram College and then studied art in Chicago and New York. Unsuccessful at various trades, he set out on a tramp-like journey across the United States, literally "singing for his supper." Today, Lindsay ranks as one of America's most outstanding and original poets. His poetry is markedly rhythmical and much of it is intended for recitation with musical accompaniment.

Henry Wadsworth Longfellow (1807–1882) is one of America's most popular poets. It is said that 15,000 copies of "The Courtship of Miles Standish" were sold on the day of its publication, and ballads like "The Wreck of the Hesperus" did much to further his fame as a poet. He resigned his professorship at Harvard in 1854 to devote himself entirely to writing. During his lifetime, honors were bestowed upon him by Cambridge and Oxford, and after his death a marble bust of him was placed in the Poet's Corner of Westminster Abbey.

Amy Lowell (1874–1925) was a member of a prominent and wealthy New England family. Many of her unconventional ideas were in sharp contrast with her conservative background. Widely read and traveled, Miss Lowell made her decision to become a poet when she was in her late twenties. Her work was published some years later but she did not enjoy critical success until the appearance of her second volume of poems, *Sword Blades and Poppy Seeds*. Like H. D. (Hilda Doolittle), Amy Lowell was an Imagist who championed the use of free verse, exact words, and new experimental techniques.

Phyllis McGinley (1905–   ) is best known for her light witty poems. In 1960 she received the Pulitzer Prize for a volume of her collected poems. In addition to her verse, she is well known for her highly popular children's books.

Don Marquis (1878–1937) won his greatest popularity as a writer of humorous stories and verses, particularly those that recount the adventures of *archy*, the literary cockroach, and his friend, *mehitabel*, the cat. A newspaper writer, whose last years were tragic ones of illness and poverty, Marquis used his two delightful little characters to make amusing and satirical comments about society and politics.

Martial, Marcus Valerius Martialis (40–104) came to Rome as a poet under the protection of the writers Seneca and Lucan. With money earned from the sale of his poems, he was able to buy a small farm and a town house in Rome. His growing disillusionment with Roman life caused him to return to his birthplace in Spain where he spent his final years living a quiet, rural existence.

Edgar Lee Masters (1869–1950) studied law at Knox College and passed his bar examination at the age of twenty-two. However, his real love was poetry, and by the time he was twenty-four, he had written almost four hundred poems. His early work is considered by some critics to be imitative of the poetry of Walt Whitman. His most famous collection of poems, *Spoon River Anthology*, a thinly veiled satire on the real people of his home town, established him as an important American poet.

Edna St. Vincent Millay (1892–1950) won recognition as a poet while still a student at Vassar College. Following her graduation, Miss Millay went to New York, determined to support herself by writing. She took up residence in Greenwich Village and helped to turn that part of New York City into a center of literary activity. The intense, romantic lyrics she wrote at that time are probably her best-known poems. In 1923, she was awarded the Pulitzer Prize for her collection of verse, *The Harp-Weaver*. Her later poems are less personal and less intense, and are concerned with graver issues than those of her youth.

R. Stanley Peterson (1905–1972) was a native of Illinois with a long period of service in secondary education. He was born in De Kalb, Illinois, received his A.B. degree from the state university and his master's degree from Harvard University. His published work has appeared in the *English Journal* and in the publications of the Yale Conference. He was editor of *Designs in Poetry*, and co-editor of the *Using Good English* series for secondary schools. He held a joint appointment between New Trier High School, Winnetka, Illinois, and Northwestern University.

Edgar Allan Poe (1809–1849) has been called the originator of the modern detective story. Born of actor parents and left an orphan at an early age, he was befriended by the merchant John Allan. Poe's career as a student at both the University of Virginia and West Point ended in failure. Forced to earn a living, he worked as an editor on various publications in which some of his own stories and poems appeared. His tales of terror have placed him high on the list of American prose writers, and his poetry often captures the same strange and melancholy mood that characterizes the tales.

Alexander Pope (1688–1744) was twenty-one when his first book of poetry, written four years earlier, was published. Poor health, as well as the religious discrimination of that time, prevented him from attending the better schools and pursuing a career in politics. By reading widely, he made up for the lack of a formal education. The brilliance of his essays and the sharp wit and satire of his poetry eventually made him the literary idol of London.

Ezra Pound (1885–1972) was born and studied in the United States but lived during most of his literary career in various countries in Europe, notably France, England, and Italy. He was one of the most influential of modern poets, although much of his major poetry was too obscure to be widely popular. He assisted many famous literary figures in their early careers. He achieved international notice when he broadcast anti–American and anti–Semitic propaganda from Italy during World War II and later was indicted in the United States for treason. Despite the questions about this part of his life, the literary quality of his works was rarely questioned and he received the Bollingen Prize for Poetry in 1949.

Lizette Woodworth Reese (1856–1935) enjoyed a successful career as a teacher yet found time to write five volumes of poetry. Her reputation among the literary figures of her time was high. She achieved distinction as the author of concise, fresh lyrics which express a genuine love of nature.

Edwin Arlington Robinson (1869–1935) was born in Head Tide, Maine, but reared in Gardiner, Maine, which was to become the "Tilbury Town" of his poetry. He attended Harvard for two years, then he was forced to leave for lack of funds. He worked for some years as a time checker for New York City subways, until he was offered a job as a clerk in the New York City customs house. By 1916, he was fully established as a poet and from that time devoted himself completely to poetry. The winning of three Pulitzer Prizes and many honors and awards for his work seemed to offer small consolation to Robinson, whose life appears to have been a lonely and unhappy one.

Carl Sandburg (1878–1967) is one of America's most distinguished poets. The son of a Swedish immigrant, Sandburg spent his youth working at a variety of odd jobs ranging from milk-truck driver to part-time fireman. On graduating from college, he became a journalist and later published several volumes of outstanding poetry. Sandburg has traveled around the country, lecturing, reading his poetry, singing folk songs, and collecting old ballads. His monumental biography of Abraham Lincoln won him a Pulitzer Prize for history in 1940. For *Complete Poems*, (1950), he received the Pulitzer Prize for literature.

Sir Walter Scott (1771–1832) was born in Edinburgh, the son of a lawyer. He was largely self-taught He became apprenticed to his father, who had urged him to study law, and was admitted to the bar. Later, he assumed two public offices which he held throughout his life. He is known for his ballads of the Scottish Border and for his many and wide ranging novels, including *Rob Roy, Ivanhoe,* and *Kenilworth.*

William Shakespeare (1564–1616) was the author of what many critics consider the greatest plays ever written in the English language. His father was a prosperous merchant as well as a prominent figure in Stratford, England, where Shakespeare was born and attended school. After his marriage, at the age of nineteen, to Anne Hathaway, Shakespeare left Stratford in search of opportunities to support his family. His theatrical career had its start when he became an actor-apprentice in London in 1593. During the next twenty years he wrote the great tragedies and comedies which brought him success in his own lifetime, and a degree of immortality that has rarely, if ever, been attained by any other poet or playwright.

Karl Shapiro (1913–   ) received little notice for his poetry until he won the Pulitzer Prize in 1945 for a collection of poems, many of which dealt with his experiences in World War II. He has continued publishing new volumes of poetry periodically, and he has taught at several universities. He is currently at the University of California at Davis.

Percy Bysshe Shelley (1792–1822) was one of the leading Romantic poets of the nineteenth century. Because of the persecution he suffered from fellow students, Shelley's days at Eton and Oxford were extremely unhappy. His poetry reflects a bitter hatred of oppression in any form, as well as a belief in the essential goodness of human nature. He lived the last years of his short life in Italy with his wife, Mary Shelley, the author of *Frankenstein.* Shelley was drowned at the age of thirty while sailing a small boat off the Italian coast.

Stephen Spender (1909–   ), an English poet, left Oxford without a degree to devote himself to a literary career. His early poems often dealt with social and political protest. His recent career has been devoted to poetry writing and literary criticism.

Wallace Stevens (1879–1955) attended Harvard and the New York University Law School before being admitted to the bar in 1904. He practiced law for a time, then in 1916 entered the legal department of the Hartford Accident and Indemnity Company of Hartford, Connecticut, eventually becoming a vice-president of the company and remaining with them until his death. His poetry received much critical acclaim and won for him the Bollingen Prize in 1949, the Pulitzer Prize in 1955, and the National Book Award in both 1951 and 1955.

Alfred, Lord Tennyson (1809–1892) began writing verse at the age of eight. The son of a minister, he received his early education from private tutors and later attended Cambridge. The publication of "Morte d'Arthur," "Ulysses," and "Locksley Hall" established Tennyson's fame as a poet, and in 1850 he succeeded Wordsworth as Poet Laureate of England. He thought and wrote upon most of the critical questions of the nineteenth century: woman's rights, economics, politics, science, and religion. His idealism and his devotion to a rather formal virtue reflect some of the basic convictions of the age in which he lived.

Louis Untermeyer (1885–   ) left high school at the age of fifteen to enter his father's jewelry business. Twenty-three years later he resigned to devote full time to writing the poetry and literary essays which brought him recognition, and to editing numerous anthologies of poetry. He has also found time to deliver countless lectures throughout the country.

Margaret Abigail Walker (1915–   ) was born in Birmingham, Alabama, daughter of a black minister. She was graduated from Northwestern University in 1935 and subsequently taught in several colleges. Her first book of poems, *For My People*, won the *Yale Younger Poets Prize* in 1942. She has received other prizes both for her poetry and a novel, *Jubilee*, published in 1966. Virtually all of her poems deal with black people.

Edmund Waller (1606–1687) became a member of Parliament at the age of seventeen. He began to write poetry during the reign of Charles I, and continued as a poet throughout the period of Cromwell and the Restoration. Walter's first volume of poetry, published in 1645, was an immediate success. Since most of his poetry was written for the special occasions that took place during his lifetime, his popularity as a poet decreased after his death. He is best remembered for the beautiful lyric "Go, Lovely Rose."

E. B. White (1899–   ) is best known as an essayist and a shrewd, witty commentator on American life. He has also written short stories, poems, and some very successful children's books.

Walt Whitman (1819–1892) saw himself as "the voice of the common man," and dedicated himself to the task of celebrating America and democracy in his poetry. Whitman grew up in Brooklyn, where he later served as printer's devil, journeyman, compositor, and traveling schoolteacher. For a time he was the editor of *The Brooklyn Eagle*. With the publication of his *Leaves of Grass*, a new and powerful force was given to American poetry. Whitman has been called the first modern American poet, for he blazed a new trail with his use of free verse and his treatment of subjects that earlier poets thought were unsuitable for poetry. He is considered one of the greatest poets America has produced.

Richard Wilbur (1921–   ) was born in New York City. He was graduated from Amherst in 1942, then spent several years in the 36th Infantry Division before receiving his M.A. from Harvard in 1947. Since then Wilbur has taught at Harvard and at Wesleyan University (Middletown, Conn.), where he is now Professor of English. In 1952, he received a Guggenheim Fellowship and in 1954 the Prix de Rome. For his volume of poems, *Things of This World*, he was awarded the Pulitzer Prize and the National Book Award for 1956.

William Carlos Williams (1883–1963) was by profession a doctor who also achieved fame as a leading American poet. Educated in both Europe and the United States, Dr. Williams spent most of his life in Rutherford, New Jersey, where he was born. His poetry, modern in content and style, is written in free-verse form, with short lines and the broken rhythms of speech.

William Wordsworth (1770–1850) spent most of his life in the Lake Country of England, a section famous for its great natural beauty. A visit to France, where he became interested in the principles of the French Revolution, and later, a visit to Germany, where he was exposed to German philosophy, had profound effects upon him. The Lake Country, however, remained the greatest influence on Wordsworth's life and poetry. Together with Coleridge, he helped usher in the Romantic Movement in poetry. One of Wordsworth's major themes is the love of nature, and the peace and contentment it can bring to man. In 1843, he was appointed Poet Laureate of England by Queen Victoria.

Elinor Wylie (1885–1928) wrote poetry from the time she was a small child but she did not begin her literary career until the age of thirty-five when her first book of poems was published. After her marriage to the poet, William Rose Benét, she worked steadily at her writing and established a reputation as a leading American poet. Her collected poems were published a few years after her death.

William Butler Yeats (1865–1939) planned to become, like his father, a painter. After three years of studying art, however, Yeats decided to devote his life to literature, a momentous decision for he became one of the major lyric poets of modern times. A man of wide interests, he was active in the Irish political movement, the Irish Literary Society, and the famous Abbey Theater, which he helped to found. Yeats was awarded the Nobel Prize for Literature in 1923. His poetry, which shows the influence of Irish myths and legends, is romantic, melodious, and has a strong mystical quality.

Note: Insufficient information prevented the editors from including a biographical sketch of Peter La Farge.

Glossary of Literary Terms

alliteration: the repetition of a consonant sound, usually at the beginning of two or more words in a line of verse:

> "He clasps the crag with crooked hands"
> —Alfred, Lord Tennyson

allusion: a reference to some person, place, or event that has literary, historical, or geographical significance.

apostrophe: a figure of speech in which words are addressed to a person or thing—absent or present—or to a personified idea, such as death, truth, or nature:

> "Swiftly walk o'er the western wave,/Spirit of Night!"
> —Percy Bysshe Shelley

assonance: the repetition in a line of verse of the same vowel sound.

> "I wandered lonely as a cloud
> That floats on high o'er vales and hills"
> —William Wordsworth

atmosphere: the general overall feeling of a literary work conveyed in large part by the setting and the mood.

ballad, folk: a narrative poem of unknown origin, meant for singing, which has been handed down orally from generation to generation.

ballad, literary: a ballad composed by a known author who consciously imitates the rhythm, rhyme scheme, and stanza form of a folk ballad.

blank verse: unrhymed verse generally written in iambic pentameter:

> "I fancied when I looked at six o'clock
> the swarm still ran and scuttled just as fast."
> —Robert Frost

cliché: an expression used so often that it has lost its freshness and effectiveness. For example: busy as a bee.

connotation: the implied or suggested meaning of a word or expression.

consonance: the close repetition of the same consonant sounds before and after different vowels, such as *splish—splash*.

couplet: two consecutive lines of verse which rhyme and are usually of equal length:

"But if the while I think on thee, dear friend,
All losses are restored and sorrows end."
—William Shakespeare

couplet, closed: a couplet containing a complete thought. A closed couplet ends with a strong punctuation mark, usually a period.

couplet, open: a couplet which forms part of a thought that is completed in following lines.

denotation: the literal dictionary meaning of a word.

dialogue: the printed conversation between two or more characters in fiction, drama, or poetry.

fable: a short tale, either in prose or poetry, that teaches a moral lesson. The characters are usually (but not invariably) animals with human qualities and speech.

figure of speech: an expression in which words are used in a nonliteral way in order to convey a forceful or vivid mental picture. For specific figures of speech, see *simile, metaphor, personification, irony, apostrophe, hyperbole.*

foot: a group of syllables in a definite pattern, containing at least one accented syllable. Here are some of the most frequently used:

an *iambic foot* consists of one unaccented syllable followed by one accented syllable (. /); for example: *becaúse, retúrn.*

a *trochaic foot* consists of one accented syllable followed by one unaccented syllable (/ .); for example: *híghèr, ánswèr.*

a *dactylic foot* consists of one accented syllable followed by two unaccented syllables (/ ..); for example: *beáutìfùl, sílèntlỳ.*

an *anapestic foot* consists of two unaccented syllables followed by one accented syllable (.. /); for example: *càvàliér, tàmbóuríne.*

a *spondaic foot* consists of two accented syllables (/ /); for example. *beéfstéak, shóeshíne.*

free verse: verse which does not conform to any fixed pattern.

hyperbole: a figure of speech employing obvious exaggeration.

"And I will luve thee still, my dear,
Till a' the seas gang dry."
— Robert Burns

image: any word, or group of words, that evokes a sensory impression.

irony: a mode of expression in which the poet says one thing but means the opposite.

lyric: any short poem that seems to be especially musical and expresses, in most instances, the poet's clearly revealed thoughts and feelings.

metaphor: a figure of speech in which two things are identified with each other; a comparison of two things without the use of *like* or *as*.

> "The sun is a huntress young"
> —Vachel Lindsay

meter: the pattern of rhythm determined by the relationships between the accented and unaccented syllables in a line of poetry. Meter is established by the repetition of a dominant foot. For example: iambic tetrameter, a line of four iambs:

> "The Child is father of the Man"
> —William Wordsworth

mood: the predominating atmosphere or feeling of a poem. For example: the mood of "When Moonlight Falls" is one of awe in the face of incredible beauty.

narrative poem: a story told in verse, not intended to be sung.

parable: a short allegorical story that is designed to convey a truth or moral lesson.

paradox: a statement which while seemingly contradictory or absurd may actually be well founded or true. For example: The country is mobilizing for peace.

quatrain: a four-line stanza.

refrain: a line or stanza repeated at intervals in a poem.

rhyme: repetition of the same (or similar) sound or sounds at the end of words. Usually, in poetry, rhyming means the ending of two or more lines with words that sound alike.

rhyme, feminine: rhyming accented syllables followed by one or more identical unaccented syllables (*drifting* and *uplifting*).

rhyme, internal: rhyme within lines of verse as well as at the ends of lines.

rhyme, masculine: rhymes consisting of single accented syllables (*long* and *song*).

rhyme scheme: the pattern in which rhymes are arranged in a poem.

rhythm: the regular rise and fall of sounds; the recurrence of a definite accent pattern in prose or poetry

simile: a figure of speech in which two objects essentially different are compared and shown to have one or more qualities in common. The comparison is usually introduced by *like* or *as*.

> "April/Comes like an idiot, babbling and strewing flowers."
> —Edna St. Vincent Millay

song: a relatively short poem in a regular metrical pattern designed to be sung.

sonnet: a poem consisting of fourteen lines, usually written in iambic pentameter and dealing with a single idea or emotion.

sonnet, Italian or **Petrarchan:** a sonnet composed of an octave (eight lines) followed by a sestet (six lines). The rhyme scheme of the octave is abba abba; that of the sestet is cde cde. Poets frequently vary the scheme of the sestet.

sonnet, Shakespearean: a sonnet composed of three quatrains and a couplet. The rhyme scheme is generally abab cdcd efef gg.

stanza: a group of lines of verse treated as a unit and separated from other units by a space.

substitution: the use of a foot different from the one regularly required by the meter.

symbol: an object that stands for, or represents, an idea. For example: a dove usually represents peace; a pair of scales is often a symbol for justice.

terza rima: a series of tercets (three-line stanza) in which the second line of each tercet rhymes with the first and third lines of the following tercet: aba, bcb, cdc, ded, etc.

tone: the feeling conveyed by the author's attitude toward his subject and the particular way in which he writes about it.

Index of Titles